"In the Spirit, In the Flesh

will be well received by the Christian person who is anxious to find his place amid a world that often stresses the themes of human fear and loneliness. Father Eugene Kennedy, in a down-to-earth way, reaches out to this person and offers reflections that not only relate to the real world but also give hope to him who is groping and searching for a deeper sense of life.

"The power of the gospel is one that demands a renewed spirit on the part of man. Father Kennedy makes clear the importance of internalized religion. He stresses the importance of the human as man lives with work and family and everyday life . . .

"That we care for others, that we risk involvement in the life of another person is perhaps an over-stressed but under-practiced Christian concern. Father Kennedy's insight is that 'the man living by the Gospels does not just do things for others, nor does he just pray for them while remaining at some distance from their troubles and hopes . . . the mystery of the Living Christ is encountered, not in transports of his soul to another world, but on the hard surfaces of meeting and making ourselves present to another person.'

"*In the Spirit, In the Flesh* is a book that will make sense to so many people as they reconsider and reapply the values they attempt to live by. Realistically, Father Kennedy recognizes the tremendous complexity and dignity of the human person. But, likewise, he acknowledges our dependence on Him who is beyond and before and with each of us. Indeed, the human and the spiritual are intimately related.

"This book is written in clear and direct language. It is practical and applicable to everyday life. It is a book that deepens our awareness of the mystery of Christ and His Church in our world today. In many way~ ⁱ⁺ ⁱ

—*The Sign*

Other Books by EUGENE C. KENNEDY

Eugene C. Kennedy

IN THE SPIRIT,
IN THE FLESH

IMAGE BOOKS
A Division of Doubleday & Company, Inc.
Garden City, New York
1972

Image Books Edition 1972
by special arrangement with Doubleday & Company, Inc.
Image Books Edition published September, 1972

CONTENTS

INTRODUCTION

I am writing this book to explore briefly the implications of the Gospels as a way of life rather than as a set of dogmatic beliefs or a strictly historical record. The most exciting part about living today—and people who do not seem so sure about it keep telling me that this is an exciting time to be alive—is that the Gospels have lost their remote and stagnated religiosity. They have been freed, by scholarship and by demand, from the air-proofed display cases of history into which they had been locked by exaggerated human reverences. The Word of God, however, has never been just an interesting artifact; it is living and true, a two-edged sword that still slices through pretense, cruelty, and the other deceptions through which we keep ourselves from growing up.

This is not a theological book in a professional sense. Nor does it do much more than begin to look at the issues involved in living our lives in the mystery of Jesus. I believe, however, that all our beautiful Christian phrases, if they have any staying power at all, must make sense in everyday life. In other words, the life of the Spirit is here and now, not at some other time or in some other place. This has to show through, then, in our human experience, even when this is broken, like so many of man's endeavors, on the wheel of pain that has revolved slowly throughout all history. Perhaps, indeed, living in Jesus shows when we weep as clearly as at any other time. Only people who have loved can cry the tears of an adult; and it is in pain and love, those two questions most important to man, that we live the Christian mystery. The Gospels suffer mightily at the hands of preachers who urge men to look be-

yond their humanity for religious experience. If the Gospels
open to us a way of life, then this world, in your life and mine,
is the immediate setting in which we can know it. The life of
the Gospels cannot be separate from our most significant human experiences—from the living and hoping, the loving and
the longing that mark our efforts to reach each other rather
than some mysterious divinity that is always just beyond us.

The theologians have come to talk of this now that the
world has made the urgent questions very clear. We hear,
for example, of incarnational theology, which tells us that the
mystery of living in Christ is encountered only by those who
seek to become fully human in this world. The theologians
are discovering what makes the human heart beat and what
breaks it too, and they know that this cannot be something
other than a share in the living and dying of Jesus. The problem comes, not from the scholars who are validating what
sensitive humans have always known about what is important
in life, but from the Church leaders who have kept up neither with the theologians nor with the struggling human family. They tend to look at this life, even the best of it, and warn
us that this is only "the natural plane" and that man's deepest
yearnings are still "merely human." Their religion still focuses
on a God who lives at a distance from the human race and
who demands a religious kind of response from man that con-
tradicts his common sense and his best hopes. The Gospels
tell us, on the contrary, that God lives very closely with man,
and that true religion challenges man to find and fulfill himself as completely as possible.

This offers hope to at least two large groups of people: first,
to those who have felt an increasing alienation from organized
religion and who may have only a tenuous relationship with
formal religious practice; secondly, to those who remain in
the Church and who find themselves increasingly discouraged
by the official Church's slowness in responding to the need
for more thoroughgoing renewal. The Gospel is good news for
these people; it speaks, better than the hesitant words of some
churchmen, to their own experience of life. The Gospels have
something to say to these people, a message at once hopeful
and sustaining. There are millions of people in these two categories, and they need to know that their questions and doubts

are good ones, that they are on the right track, and that they will outlast the timorous who think that the good news is bad news, or seem to, anyway, because they are so reluctant to preach it to anyone. Healthy people, acutely aware of what constitutes the heart of real living, need to know that their instincts are fundamentally correct: religion has to do with life, not ceremony or power; it has to do with man's freedom to be himself, not with controlling his every move.

In a sense, this is meant to be a responsive and practical book that helps people to recognize the dimensions of the truly religious experiences which they have every day. If we live in the mystery of Jesus, then we should be able to recognize the life experience in which this is revealed to us. Otherwise religion is only wishful thinking, the psychological projection of our infantile needs across the skies, and all our talk about the living experience of Christianity is more a strenuous exercise of the imagination than anything in which we can really believe.

What do we do about this reality of the Gospel life? Are our experiences with each other substantial enough to bear the weight of the redemptive significance they possess if the Gospels are good news? We can only find out by testing this experience, sounding the depths of our struggles to grow and to love one another by living intensely in this world instead of waiting for another one. I hope that these reflections will help people who take this life seriously to enter it more deeply and to know, in the heart of their deepest human searches, that they do live, suffer, and find new life in and through Jesus.

I think that the more we grow into adult Christians who are sure of the center of gravity of our faith in our own human experience, the more the structures of the Church themselves will change. This may not make any difference to people who no longer find themselves interested in the forms of religious institutions. Restructuring may be an aggravating rather than an exciting concept to the Christians who are weary of the arguing and the anxiety that have marked the recent history of the Church. Indeed, it is today somehow darkly fashionable to speak of the death of various forms of institutionalized Christianity: the parish, the religious order, and in general, our hopes for a renewed Church. This vocabulary of death makes us misunderstand our present experience; those who speak these words emphasize the dying in a distorted way, reveling in it almost, like grim cynics sipping champagne with the enemy at the gates. The truth, however, lies in a corrected perception of the contemporary resurrection experience, the surge of vitality unshackled by the passing away of certain religious forms of expression. It is this coming to life that is the sign of our hope for a renewed and more humanly responsive Church. The new Church will take its shape from the Christians who believe in life rather than death, from the Christians who keep working at building a better servant community on the basis of the Gospels.

This is a book, then, for hopeful people who want to live the Gospel life and who want to help others to understand and to share it. It is to light up their way a little, to offer them encouragement, and through them to give back to the world the Gospel of hope that I write this book.

Eugene C. Kennedy
F.S.

IN THE SPIRIT, IN THE FLESH

1. AFTER OUR MYTHS HAVE DIED

Man has never viewed the future with so much interest and so little hope. Experts, weighed down with computer printouts, arch a shower of mathematical growth curves over the edge of the coming century; others, like Camus, hear the stirrings of man's spirit and invite him to look into the tragic night of the future with courage but without much hope. The twenty-first century glows dimly but clearly on the horizon of time. Some observers see men striving to reach the shore of a new and better age; others say that men, like the unknowing crew of the *Californian*, curious but passive to the *Titanic*'s flares, understand neither their voyage nor its opportunities.

Man is dealing with his meaning at the present time, sorting out the myths which have explained life to him through the centuries. He discards those which no longer bear the weight of his experience but he also searches for a new and sustaining myth to support him into the future. In this context we can see the opportunity of the churches to speak again to man, in the language of myth that has always been so significant in transmitting religious truths, about the most important things in life, the very things men seem hardly able to speak about any more.

There is an obvious problem in speaking about myth and its transcendent vocabulary. The popular connotation of the word myth is misleading. Myths do not refer only to fables or fairy stories. Neither are they the blemish-free images conjured up by TV political campaigns that loom larger than the political candidate they represent. Myths, in fact, offer us a way to tell the truth. The language of myth is a special mode of communication through which man preserves his values and beliefs and hands them on to future generations. Myth is a powerful symbolic language that conveys the truth more sharply than do facts or photographs. Man employs myths when he wants to transcend time and to preserve the richest human insights from the ravages of the instant historians. Mytho-poetic language is not a vehicle for falsehood or delusion but for the truth. Myths hold the truth for us in the way that the great artists always have, by selecting and emphasizing certain features of our experience with the special vision that is reserved for the deeply sensitive. You can tell more truth about man and his world with a good myth than you can with an encyclopedia.

The signs of man's interest in myth are all about us. They are not the gathering biblical signs that Dr. Billy Graham takes so literally with fire, lightning, disconsolate wailing, and the end of the world waiting in the wings. Man's myths sometimes employ that kind of dramatic imagery but they do point to more than climactic or judgmental events. They refer just as much to what goes on in man in his everyday struggles to live and to love in a genuinely human way. They tell about man as he seeks to become fully himself. It is about the mysteries connected with these commonplace but deeply human activities that men long to speak both to themselves and to others in our time. Like the suffering patient in psychotherapy, modern men search for the words that let them truly experience themselves; they long for the symbols that can only be given to them by other persons who have traveled deeply and sensitively into the farthest regions of human experience. Myth, when it is well used, is a psychotherapeutic language because it symbolizes and integrates for man the deepest aspects of his human experience. Good myth is a language of wisdom. Two modern writers illustrate this in their attempts to interpret events. It is of man's estrangement from healing and meaningful myths that existential therapist Rolla May writes. It is in the very language of myth that Yale Professor Charles Reich tries to provide a vision of hope for modern man.

May sees man's hopelessness as the cold inner echo of the

alienation which he feels because he has lost touch with the human truth-telling power of the myths that have guided him for years. Man has lost his potent vocabulary of myth, the language he has always used to speak to himself and to other men about the wellsprings of the human spirit. It has been replaced by another language, the efficient language of mathematics upon which computers feed, the language of gross national products and Dow-Jones averages, the language that suffocates men because you cannot use it to say "I love you." The deep wound of alienation, the plaguing feeling of being a stranger in a land where nothing is familiar, must be healed, according to May, if man is to survive into the next century. The healing will take place only if man can find again the language that enables him to understand and share with others his many sided humanity.

Reich, in his book *The Greening of America* attempts, unconsciously and incompletely, to restore man's language of myths, to give him back a way of talking again about the human values that seem so repressed at this time in history. He writes of his vision, right or wrong, to the people who want to be able to hope again, the millions who hurt so much in the present and who long for a redeeming future. He offers a mytho-poetic vision of man resurrected through a new Consciousness III, as he terms it, that will make the desert landscape of modern America bloom again. He looks to the young, with their concern about personal values and public honor, for salvation. Reich's book, reviewed because of some of its content by many economists, is hardly a book about economics at all. It is a book about man and his longings, and, in a very inexact and romantic way, Reich proclaims the new myth that will save us from the dangers of technology. He puts deliverance in the hands of the young, believing that their goodness, truthfulness, and beauty will reorder the priorities of our culture. What he is really writing about, of course, is the fact that there is a positive reservoir in man, good things still beneath the scarred human condition, and that only a return to these will see us across the threshold of the year 2000. Of course, it is not a book of economics; it is a book of myth, telling in a new way the old truth about man's spiritual needs and possibilities.

May and Reich, among many others, constitute the signs of the times to which the Church should pay attention. They are defining in the powerful language of myth rather than the legal language of heresy the great contemporary religious problems of man. They are prophets of a kind, indicating that somebody with the truth about man must talk to him again in a language that he can understand. It is curious that man's needs should be described in mythological language just at the time that the Church is discovering that it has been using this language for centuries without fully realizing it. In fact, it has misunderstood it at times, trying to tease literal meaning out of what was symbolic and insisting on making history out of words that were intended to convey timeless truths.

Now the scholars of the Church, liberated from earlier twentieth-century Roman restraints on their research, are examining the mytho-poetic language in which the great messages of Jesus have been preserved for us in the Gospels. This does not, of course, mean that there is no historical truth in them; it does point to the fact, however, that although they are written in the symbols and imagery of the culture of their day their meaning is not tied down to one point in history. So scripture scholars, like skilled psychotherapists, try to get beneath the language and expressions of the ancient authors and to understand, in terms of the writers' times, customs, and limitations, exactly what they were attempting to put down. The Gospels tell of man's meaning and relationship to God; they exhaust the historical storyteller's arts in the process. The Church, in other words, through the work of its theologians and scripture scholars, is learning to speak again the language of salvation, the very myth that men want and need to hear.

A renewed understanding of the language of the Gospel increases rather than diminishes our faith. What is expected of man and the way he lives with himself and others is far more compelling when we get a fresh view of Christ's teaching through a more sensitive appreciation of Gospel style. Faith is meant for the whole man; it does not demand merely intellectual assent to certain propositions, nor the unquestioning acceptance of certain historical phenomena. Faith is much grander than that. Faith gets at a man's vitals, challenging him to change his ways and to enlarge his life even at the price of losing it. All the wonder and startling challenge of Jesus' message to mankind come straight out of the Scriptures when we are attuned to the mytho-poetic character of much of their content. In fact, the Gospel is the guiding myth for which men are searching, the response to man's painful alienation, the promise, not fulfilled by magical confidence in youth, that man can make sense of it all, that he can grow and redeem himself. The Gospels are the myth that tells us of our life with God, a life in which we are caught up with our fellow men in the mysteries of incarnation, death, and resurrection which encompass all our days. The Gospels are the new language that says we cannot save ourselves except we be friends with one another, that salvation lies beneath the ordinary faces of believing in, hoping for, and loving each other. The Gospels are the myth that tells us that we are made to live forever.

The Church, in other words, has now a very real opportunity to open the Scriptures anew to men, not as historical documents or as catalogues of intellectual beliefs, but as the powerful force to transform their lives and to give them a new and integrated sense of themselves and the world in which they live. Men need the truth that gives them back an understanding of their own significance and a new chance to participate in life as individual, loving persons. The rediscovery of the Gospels, with the welter of superfluous wonders peeled away, is the language that men have been waiting to hear again. The Gospels offer men the chance, not to be gods, but truly and fully to be men. And this is the point of the Christian life.

Some overeager progressives will seize on what has been unfortunately called the demythologization of the Gospels to shred every sacred intuition out of them. The world surely needs those who can demythologize the Gospels. The process, however, is not accomplished by subtracting from their meaning as much as through interpreting on a deeper level what their genuine meaning is. As the shadows of the next century already fall across our calendars, this is the biggest challenge the Church has; indeed, it is its most important business. This is a difficult task, of course, but one that has urgency for all men, not merely for special scholars or for those with the proper credentials of Church membership. Mankind cannot have hope unless the values of the life of the Spirit are presented in the context of a saving way of life rather than as a rigid and humanly estranging code of conduct or as the product of hopelessly neurotic fancy.

These latter descriptions do, in fact, tell us what has happened to religion in the last few centuries. It is coming to life again in our time because man hurts in that part of his personality where he wants to believe. Only a new and a more fully developed religious vision can help him. A renewed Gospel does tell men about life; it echoes in their own experience and cuts, with living force, across their consciences. When proclaimed clearly, the Gospels are a source of the Spirit for men who are trying to find their way. The Gospels are powerful and they can change men, not by manipulating them, but by opening up to them the possibilities of true growth. Church officials can never make this power of the Spirit available to men until they themselves relearn the language of Gospel myth and put aside the exercise of personal and political power which has often obscured their understanding of the power of the Spirit.

To enter into the rich mytho-poetic world of the Gospels we have to be able to allow other and lesser myths to die or to be retired. Renewal might be understood as a process of casting off the failed myths of the past and replacing them with the valid and reliable ones that come from the Scriptures themselves. There are many layers of mythology in the Christian churches; the Roman Catholic Church, as the oldest of them all, is practically hidden by the vine-like growth of the centuries. But how can a person tell one myth from another, or when a myth no longer serves the truth, or when it is time to discard it? How can we be sure that the new language of myth is reliable? The answer is not just in careful scholarship, although this is vitally important. The answer to all these comes out of the test of myth in the everyday life of the Christian who seeks to live by the Spirit. This is the test of experience that cuts through what is insubstantial and false more surely than anything else. Ultimately, the only way we can sort out the valid Christian myths from the invalid ones is to see whether they do, in fact, promote man's growth in the essential qualities of the Christian life. The depth of a myth is sounded in the hearts of men who resonate to the truth which matches their nature and helps them to grow toward its fullness.

The strength of the enduring myths cannot be understood unless we are prepared to put aside the outworn and inadequate myths that have, in effect, delayed the maturing of Christian faith considerably. Perhaps the most overblown of all these myths is the one that has exalted the position and authority of Church officials at the expense of the developing autonomy of man himself. Nothing has done greater disservice to man's growth as a Christian person than the habit of mind which made him passive and dependent on inflated and controlling churchmen. Only the timid, or those who fear the loss of influence, reject the possibility of re-examining our guiding myths outright. But men became alienated from the Church because so many Church spokesmen forgot the language of the Gospels and could speak only in the crippling myths that perpetuated their own prestige and their own position to supervise the lives of the members of the Church. There is an old Eskimo saying about their unchanging folklore: "We tell stories in the same words so that we can live untroubled." This catches the flavor of the fearful who are unwilling to reorganize their world or their beliefs on the basis of a new and richer understanding of the meaning of the Gospel. This is the attitude that has strengthened the old-time religion, that powerful and immature mythology that falls so short of truth about God and man, the caricature of religion that has estranged man from its true meaning.

It is time to face some of our more encrusted Catholic mythologies and to scrape them loose from our lives for good. This is in the best interest of a renewing Church but it is more important as a service to the world itself. If ever there was a time to return to the purity of the Gospel message it is now. The human situation is desperate and men are tired of theological wrangling and ivory tower theologizing. They want something to hold on to, truths to live by, but they must hear them in a language that touches and transforms them with the power of the Spirit. Men want to know how to live according to the teachings of the Gospel and whether and how these have relevance to their everyday lives. They want to do the right thing, most of them, and they need the assistance of the Gospel truth more than a code of canon law to do this. Men want to reach each other, to explore the mysterious interpersonal territory of hope and trust, and to learn to love in lasting fashion. Men want to understand, if they can, why things go wrong, why life has so many tragedies, and why their days are scored by loneliness and death. Men want a reliable interpretative scheme that will enable them to take control of their own lives with a sense of their own significance. They are weary of the cautionary and demanding net that some have thrown over them in the name of religion. Above all, men want something positive, something through which they can achieve resurrection despite the crucifixions that fill this life. Men want and are willing to pay the price of honesty for the ultimately freeing truth about themselves and the life that the Gospels preserve in their potent mytho-poetic style.

The Gospel is meant to be available to every man; it invites us to a way of life rather than to an intellectual exercise. It is powerful, the strength of the Spirit welling out of its words to illumine and transform us by making us sense the reality of our own incorporation into Christ. The Gospels comfort us but they lay down the challenge to live differently in a way that no other book does. The Gospels replace beneath our feet the ground which Bonhoeffer said had been cut away by the churches that had become strangers to the Gospels.

After all the new manuals of theology are finally written, the same old questions will plague the average man. He really does not want technical explanations of the nature of myth; he just wants to know how to live. The best myths, then, are not self-conscious ones, but those whose power comes from their profound human appropriateness, from their rootedness in the human condition. For the life of the Spirit is lived in that human condition. Its goal, as the theologians are at long last realizing, is the complete development of man. What, then, contributes to man's growth as man? How, once the time-honored assertion is made, can he be himself? What, at the heart of good Christian myth, is the manner of healing alienation without descending to the moralizing extrinsic formulas of the past? The Christian life, in other words, must be more than beautiful sounding; it must be fundamentally possible and its vision must be available to all. The Christian myth does not promise pie in the sky. It promises fuller life right now. We must avoid translating all our troubles into mytho-poetic language, as though that were enough in itself.

The most important things to investigate, then, are the psychological conditions and consequences for man as he lives the life of the Spirit. If it is not magic, then how does it work? What happens inside a person when he grows in the Spirit, how can he understand it, and what can he do to promote it? The questions come down to asking what is the human underside of the myths that say we must die in order to live, that we can all be friends, and that we can make a community together? What, in our innards, does love, the high point of Christian life, ask of and do to us? I think that unless we explore these questions we will have laid hold in the renewed Gospel of only an intellectualized Christian myth, one that, because we do not understand its personal dimensions, will be powerless to transform our lives. The true Kingdom preached by Jesus is profoundly human in its foundations. After all the other thundering questions of this theological high noon are settled, we will still have to confront the challenge of what the Gospels mean as a way of life for each of us.

2. LEADERLESS CHRISTIANITY

Bonhoeffer had it wrong; Christianity has not come to a phase without religion as much as to a time without leaders. It is probably true to say that we have never had a surplus of inspiring official leaders, although we have longed for them and, because of a combination of wishful thinking and an authoritarian tradition, we have treated such leaders as we have had as something not much less than the angels. This reflects an earlier and less developed sense of religious faith in which all externals, leaders included, were necessarily more important at times than the substance of Gospel faith itself. I suggest, however, that Christianity has been growing and that it is the hand of the Spirit rather than the devil that one can see in all this. The growth in a richer and deeper faith has shifted the center of gravity of belief in our day from things outside of us to the internal forum where conscience and choice meet to shape religious response. This development of faith in numberless sincere individuals has inevitably made them less dependent on outside authority and externals for the nourishment and expression of their Christian beliefs.

The face of this dynamic of growth looks like and is interpreted as a challenge to the authority of Church leaders. You can document this view with a thousand headlines about conscience over encyclicals, rebellious priests, and religious and hand-wringing ecclesiastics who find that people no longer dance readily to their piping. This dangerous misinterpretation is based on a faulty understanding of what is happening as well as a preadolescent fixation about the role of authority. The notion, in other words, that the authority of the Church is crumbling is a false myth which, however, many people, including Church authorities at times, employ to guide their lives. This dramatic misreading of the signs of the times makes for good feature stories but it ignores the widespread longing for and achievement of a deepened religious faith which has placed authority in a new and healthier perspective in the Church.

Whenever a man deepens his faith he necessarily separates himself somewhat from the institutional forms of his religious affiliation. If he lives from an internalized faith he simply does not need so many external props to support his belief. In the normal process of internalizing his faith he has tested the religious truths given to him in childhood against his experience of life itself. This brings him up against the hard questions of what and why he believes and whether he will make his faith his own as the inner core from which his life and behavior spring. If he does this, he puts aside many of those things which he needed in the childhood of his religious faith precisely because they now impede rather than serve him in his free response to the Spirit. This is not to say that the externals of faith no longer have significance for him; they do, but only insofar as they effectively point beyond themselves to the realities of the Gospel life.

Autonomy of faith, relief from within rather than because of pressure from without, the liberated embrace of the teachings of Christ: these are perennial goals of religious education and formation. Man is meant to burn himself free of the dross of self-deception and to move beyond magic and superstition as he journeys to the far and lonely reaches of adult and independent faith. We should, therefore, expect to find Christians searching themselves very seriously about the content and implications of their belief in this day. We can hardly be surprised to discover that persons growing in their faith, like persons growing in any way in life, want to take responsibility for themselves and are not content to believe or act just because somebody else tells them to do so in a prescribed and presumably authority-blessed manner. To wish to live without minutely detailed rules is not an affront to authority as much as it is an impulse toward mature Christian living. It is an affront to persons on the part of some authorities when

they keep insisting on this kind of control of individual behavior.

On a massive scale, perhaps for the first time in history,
men are evidently moving toward this deepened kind of
faith. The crisis connected with this is not a symptom of ter-
minal illness in Christianity but rather an indication of renewing vitality. This crisis may, as some worried Church
leaders have described it, be one of faith but it is not one of
belief. Immature faith, its inconsistencies and shallowness
showing through, is fragmenting; along with it, of course, goes
all the baggage of authoritarian mythologies. The present situation signifies not a loss of faith as much as a transformation
of the quality of men's religious faith. As it develops, faith
becomes more demanding, not for abject response to external
authority, but for willing obedience to the internal voice of
the Spirit. There is no lack of belief, only a more urgent quest
for something that is truly worth believing in, for the kind of
faith that matches the true depths of human personality. People who are upset by the tension within contemporary religious institutions fail to see this as a reflection of men's readi-
ness for a more refined and internalized religious faith. This
growth toward Christian self-determination necessarily challenges the style and exercise of authority in religious organiza-
tions which are built on a less developed style of faith.

Zbigniew Brzezinski has recently written of this phenomenon in what he calls the "age of volatile belief" (*Between
Two Ages, America's Role in the Technetronic Era*, The Vi-
king Press, New York, 1970). Noting polls which indicate
lower attendance at church and decreased acceptance of traditional beliefs in God, he writes:

> . . . it would be misleading to conclude that low church
> attendance and disbelief in life after death mean per-
> vasive irreligiosity. On the contrary, it suggests that au-
> thentic irreligiosity—that is to say, a deeply felt rejection
> of a reality beyond the finite—does not exist, or at least
> not yet. A belief in God to which one cannot give sub-
> stance may merely be a holdover from a more traditional
> society in a context that emphasizes immediate life, but

it could also reflect the search for a highly personal, inner, and direct relationship between the individual and God (p. 90).

Brzezinski goes on to note that:

> . . . the waning of the Church as an institution may be a symptom of intensifying religiosity. The Church was a necessary intermediary between God and man in the phase of man's spiritual poverty and historical unawareness. It provided a rigid code of behavior, institutionalized sanctions (which gradually declined in severity as mankind was socialized on the level of personal, though not international, coexistence), and a link to the eternal. As the Church fades, for some the disintegration of its controls will doubtless mean license; for many it will simply be a matter of indifference; but for others it will be the beginning of a much more direct, more personal, less ritualized relationship with God (pp. 90, 91).

The renewal of the Catholic Church can, in fact, be understood as the effort of the world's oldest institution to modify itself so that it can better express and strengthen an internalized religious faith while, at the same time, it maintains some kind of institutional integrity. With rare exceptions, the leaders of the Church have shown little sensitivity to this reality and, despite their votes at Vatican II, they have been more frightened at the prospect of losing their controlling authority than anything else. This is hardly to be wondered at, given the fact that most of the bishops of the Church were promoted to their present positions because of their steadfast support and loyal service to the ecclesiastical institution. They also represent a generation of leaders caught up in and sustained by a narrow, monarchical interpretation of the episcopal office that has provided more burdens than boons for them and their people.

We are only beginning to see some of the long cherished notions of the development of the office of the bishop clarified by competent scholarship, such as that of Father Raymond Brown in his remarkable book *Bishop and Priest* (The

Paulist Press, 1970). Weighed down with the mythology of a "fullness of the priesthood" and a sense of position bolstered by the notion that their power has come directly to them from the original twelve apostles, the bishops have had an inflated impression of their own role and their own capacities as teachers and leaders. This sounds like a strong indictment of good-willed and hard-working men; in a sense, it is.

In another sense, however, it merely opens the way for us to see how we strangle faith and actually destroy authority when we invest it with too many prerogatives. Until the bishops of the Church can redefine their own self-concept and place themselves again within some style of reasonable relationship to their people, they will continue to misunderstand and, in general, react ineffectively to the religious crises of the day. This will only frustrate and disappoint many of them who will realize that they are not making the Church run the way it used to and who will blame themselves or a lack of faith in their priests and people for the situation. They will not be able to understand, as long as they think that everything depends on them, the enormous changes in religious faith, most of them beyond their control, that are occurring in the contemporary world. In other words, the more they try to control the Church through the exercise of their distorted sense of episcopal power, the more clearly they will emerge as administrators made distressingly vulnerable by the age's need for genuine leaders. With a deepening religious faith motivating men toward more independence of judgment about the imperatives of Gospel faith, and with bishops unfortunately trapped in a narrowly defined range of administrative expectations, the committed Christian realizes that he has entered the era of leaderless Christianity.

This tragedy, naturally, is made worse by the fact that we so desperately do need Church leaders who can inspire us, even if they have to know how to read balance sheets as well as how to preach the Gospels. It is a melancholy conclusion to state that the bishops of the Roman Catholic Church are, in general, the individuals who have been least affected by the renewal experience of the Church. This would not be the first time that such a phenomenon has occurred, nor is the bishopric the only occupation ever to be affected by it.

Old generals, admirals, and judges also have a hard time understanding and responding to the experience of change in their private worlds because they have led such successfully insulated lives. Most bishops have preserved prestige, the exercise of power, and the privacy of their own personal chapels throughout the tumultuous years since Vatican II. Their personal and devotional lives have remained pretty much intact. They have seldom had the kinds of experiences that, on a deeply personal level, their priests and religious have known. Other supports have protected them from these. Power, even for bishops who don't profess to want it, is a great substitute for human relationships. It is, therefore, genuinely difficult for them to appreciate the intense self-search about faith and human relationships which has characterized the lives of so many priests and religious. It is all the more difficult for them to enter into the experience of their lay people. The bishops are indeed good men, squirming restlessly in their leather chairs for a better way to do things, but they are handicapped by isolation, a disease most of them do not suspect they have but whose secondary gains they prize. They are hurt by many of the things that happen in the Church because the trap they live in, like the sack Pope John said he lived in at the Vatican, leaves them little freedom of movement. They must support the institution, and, that in the argot of the day, is simply not where it is as far as the development of true religious faith goes in our world. The bishops are committed, in other words, to reinforce institutional forms which actually need flexibility built into them if they are to be vehicles and instruments of religious experience in our day.

One can feel great compassion for religious leaders, born out of due time, saddled with debts, and plagued with doubts about the Church's present and future. But, inexorably, the question comes to this: just how genuinely have the bishops themselves been pursuing a more internalized religious faith? This is a very different question from asking how piously a bishop prays or even how many hours he spends reading the Scriptures or reciting the breviary. Indeed, these activities probably have little to do with the essential aspects of religious behavior. Most of the bishops, after all, were trained to the goal of individual sanctity, to respect for regulations, to a faith summed up and secure in Church teachings. These are, interestingly enough, often the marks of an externalized faith, one clearly riddled with paradox. The individual, according to this model of spiritual development, was exalted as far as the pursuit of holiness was concerned; now many bishops resist the respect for individual conscience that presumably should have been a part of their previous ideal. There are, however, deeper questions about the faith of our leaders which must be asked if we are to understand how truly we must be able to live without them.

A better question, for example, centers on the bishops' inability to let their people and their priests move out from their close control. One can only wonder at their marked reserve about experimentation, as though any alteration might bring the Church down in ruin about them. One worries also about their faith when the supervision of people rather than the freedom of people is of such paramount concern to them. But the struggle cannot be with the bishops and their shortcomings at this time: that would be to misunderstand the nature of leaderless Christianity. Those people who continue to make the battle with the bishops the center of the stage of Christian renewal are acting out a drama that reinforces the position of the bishops as those on whom everything else depends. Very little depends on them in a church that is truly responsive to the Spirit. The Christian faith, the Gospel truths cannot be so contingent on bishops for their effectiveness. That, of course, is not to say that they are unimportant or that genuine leadership from them would not be applauded and, indeed, responded to with enthusiasm. Christians would like their bishops to be leaders, to be the men of vision that their title as overseers of the Church implies. There are just very few of them and the horizon does not seem to be teeming with charismatic successors to the present generation of bishops. The facts are that, if we are truly pursuing the Gospel ideals, then we must be strong enough to live without the leadership we might otherwise long to have. That, in fact, is an element of a developed kind of religious faith; there is a lonely quality to it at times, a stepping forward out of the secure shadows so that each of us is tested in the harsh limelight of life itself. It would indeed be supportive to have sufficient religious leaders to help us make this forward step more confidently. But we must make it anyway, even if it seems to detach us from the relationship with Church authorities that we would like to preserve. It is much like the inevitable separation children must make from their parents if they are truly to be adults themselves.

One fact is becoming clear in the present age: the Gospels and the Christian faith are strong enough to exert their spiritual force in the lives of people independently of the strength of Church leadership. Jesus' teachings are available to men whether they are articulated clearly by ministers of religion or not. And religious faith is not a colorful web of fancy that must be protected from strong winds of doubt and suffering by authorities who are afraid that it will otherwise blow away. Instead it occupies a central and integrating function in human personality; its roots run deep beneath the contradictions of the human condition and it endures in the battered heart of man even when religious institutions and religious leaders fail to express it adequately.

When religious leaders, such as bishops, think that the preaching of the Gospel or the life of the Spirit depends too much on them, then they assume a snare of responsibility for the faith which is roughly equivalent to the attitudes of overprotective parents who try to live their children's lives for them. Everybody ends up unhappy that way, the children crippled because they have been so shielded, the adults frustrated and sometimes heartbroken because they cannot successfully lead their own and other people's lives. The bishops would free themselves of a crushing sense of obligation if they could move away from the present model of over-all control and responsibility for the theory and practice of the Christian faith. This burden is just catching up with many Church leaders. I recall the distinguished archbishop with whom I dined recently. I asked him, "What is the hardest part about being archbishop?" He paused a moment, put down his fork, and said, "Four o'clock in the morning. Four o'clock when I wake up and see all the people who want answers and decisions seated on the edge of my bed . . . and I cannot get back to sleep again." He went on to describe how hurt he is when people expect him to do the impossible. A young priest, in his office to tell him that he was resigning, had accused him that very afternoon with the charge, "You sit there and you do *nothing!*" But, of course, there is so little that a prelate can do about so many problems that lie beyond his influence.

Surely this kind of human burden is too much to impose on any leader; it is surely excessive in Christianity which champions individual responsibility and nowhere portrays the elders of the Church as totally responsible—or totally competent. The enlarged mythology of the episcopate has actually weakened rather than strengthened it, placing bishops, as it does, in a vise of expectation which squeezes the life out of them. It is no wonder that they have become adept at ruling through regulations rather than through human relationships. They have had to do this to preserve their sanity, to cope with the psychological pressures that inevitably come to those who are afflicted with mistaken identity.

It simply does not make sense to imagine that a religion that is aimed at enlarging man, at freeing him to be responsible for his own salvation in the sight of God, should have tangled itself, Laocoön-like, in authoritarian directives. This goes counter to the dynamic of internalized faith, perpetuating spiritual childhood rather than bringing individuals to fullness of life in Christ. The Gospel life is far more demanding than the model of Christianity which so securely ordered one's path through life's mine field of sins and temptations. The life we learn about in the Gospels is no simple thing, no easily won salvation, because its setting is life itself and it is worked out in a painful and exhausting fashion. People who listen to the Spirit and who try to live by what he asks are not trying to get out of something when they feel a certain independence from Church authorities. They are, on the contrary, taking on something that demands self-sacrifice and constant freely chosen discipline.

One may raise the question, "Isn't an external kind of faith the best that most people can hope for? And isn't an authoritarian Church important to guide the lives of these people?" That is a fair question but, given the world-wide evidence of more people thirsting for a durable faith, it would seem dangerous, not to say scandalous, if the Church could not respond to them. It is an easy goal to treat people like children all their lives; it is far more difficult to assist them to grow, especially when this means they will grow away from you. Either the Church is in the business of helping people to fuller growth, to the achievement of a mature mode of Christian living, or it sells itself and its vocation short, shutting its eyes to need as well as opportunity. This does not mean that individuals whose faith has not become deepened should be ridiculed for their devotions or beliefs. That would be unchristian in the most profound sense, but that attitude of understanding does not absolve us from the more fundamental obligation of being agents of a deepened growth in faith for all people. The temptation is to wish that people still had the same old difficulties with religious faith, the problems reflected in the cruel aphorisms of another generation. For example, there was the familiar assertion that you either had the faith or you did not. Faith is undeniably a gift but it hardly arrives capriciously, like good weather or good looks, from some realm outside ourselves. That was a great saying, however, but one that penalized persons with problems of believing because it tended to write them off as having missed faith for some reason or other. Faith is, however, available to all, or we have made God into an inconstant and therefore unfaithful controller of our lives. Faith does not fall like the rain; it grows, changes shape, and blossoms, but it always draws its strength from the ever-available Spirit. The only thing that can make faith look like a sometime thing is the activity of humans who interfere with the action of the Spirit. The same thing applies to other old adages, such as the famous ones about young Catholics going away and losing their faith. Actually, research shows that loss of faith has some relationship to family stability, but, presuming that a young student might have discovered new questions about the old truths during his college years, it is not helpful to talk of "losing" the faith. More than likely such a person, if he was a sincere inquirer, would have run into Church spokesmen who tried to settle his doubts by rational argument and who were insensitive to the developing nature of authentic religious faith. In any case, faith cannot be successfully oversimplified to fit the absolute categories of a religious institution.

One need not despise the past to recognize the undeveloped quality of the religious faith which was handed on to so many millions of people. This approach tended to exalt and expand the mythologies connected with the levels of leadership in the Church. It did not promote the development of the religious faith as a total human experience in the members of the Church; it reinforced their acceptance of certain supposedly final interpretations of Scripture and tradition as well as decisions about personal behavior. This was the high point of the institutionalization of extrinsic religion. It has broken apart in our day and age because better educated and more self-understanding man looks for something more than an anti-intellectual and dependent kind of faith.

One witnesses a simple example of the contrast between external faith and a more inquiring type across today's generations on compulsory attendance at Sunday Mass. The older generation, obedience to this rule bred into their very bones, is made very uneasy by a younger generation that challenges an automatic and unthinking acceptance of this obligation. The older people know that there is something to the idea that man should worship God freely and that attending Mass out of fear is not a very lofty motive. They cannot, however, erase their uneasiness about letting people really be free. They think it is safer, more respectable, more symbolic of faith, even when that faith is not very substantial, for people to perform their obligation unquestioningly. Older people feel very good when their children continue to go to Mass even when they know that Mass has little meaning for them. Some older people are branded beyond healing with the mark of external religious practice.

The younger generation, on the other hand, questions an easily accepted faith and wonders about religious services which do not seem to speak very effectively to them. It is common for many of them, still deeply religious, to believe in the Eucharist but choose to fulfill their obligation on a day other than Sunday. They are incapable of taking seriously a part of their obligation which was generated and supported by the styles of externalized religious faith. They are not all-knowing or all-wise either, of course, and they frequently have little to put in place of their now deserted old-time faith. Exulting in what seems to be a never-ending now, they seem to know what they don't like even when they do not pursue very energetically a deeper kind of religious faith and practice. But, then, few people are trying to help them develop a more profound religious faith. Teachers who attempted it are given little support for their efforts. Both generations are actually challenged to take a step beyond where they are now and to build institutions and models of religious practice which are better capable of bearing man's weight and expressing the religious dimensions of personality.

If superstition and magic no longer suffice, and if the invitation to the life of the Spirit is independent of the quality of our leaders, then men must take seriously the invitation to discover the true depth of religious faith. If a religion that provided all the answers no longer evokes a response from healthy people, then it is time for man to follow out his new questions as far as he can, knowing that he can never really fail in his journey when he is looking for the truth. Now, in this trembling moment of opportunity when people are indeed looking for something solid to believe in, the churches can join men in the earnest search for the sacred dimensions of life and for a surer grasp of the way the Spirit operates in this world.

The crisis of our age is not the acceptance or rejection of faith in some absolute way; it is rather the more painful process of growing in faith, of maturing in belief where it truly touches all aspects of the human person. There is much suffering and confusion inevitable in the effort to bridge this kind of gap which is now opened wide between the childhood of man and the young adulthood of the human race. Man can make a new choice about the principles by which he will or will not live in the next century. This is, of course, related to man's ever present search for meaning and wholeness, his quest for love in some true form, and for a mankind of deepened maturity which, in its new freedom, can fulfill all of man's potential.

3. THE PROBLEM OF BEING YOURSELF

The Christian's biggest problem does not sound complicated but it is. Being yourself seems easy enough, a relief, in fact, for people worn down by the pressures of always having to pretend. But being yourself involves much more than the simple letting go of restraints that the overvirtued long for; neither is it the surrender of all struggle in favor of a passive ride on the tide of life. Being yourself implies going more deeply into ourselves, laying hold of the truth of our personality even when it has lain half buried for years, and then committing ourselves to that truth as genuinely as possible. This is a hard business, filled with unsuspected but ever recurring pressures, seeded with the kind of pain and joy that go with serious living, founded in the death-resurrection mystery that pervades all of life. There is, in fact, no way to live the life of the Spirit except in and through our own personality. The prime mythic gospel truth is that salvation comes to those who are themselves.

The forces of externalized religion have placed a great premium on the appearance of things and have shunned rather than explored the depths of man. Two of the least attractive but most powerful features of extrinsic religious faith are (1) a misperception and mistrust of human personality; (2) a willingness to settle for the hypocritical pursuit of an exterior style of so-called perfection. Modern men have protested the crippling effects of these distortions on them and their lives. They have rejected the forces and forms that have reinforced and sustained the expectations of externalized religion. Necessarily they have, in their search for something more human

and therefore more intrinsically religious, seemed irreligious
according to the standards of the shallow beliefs from which
they have tried to free themselves. Man cannot truly be himself and be extrinsically religious; we are watching him work
his way out of this uncomfortable dilemma at the present
time.

According to the first distortion of an immature religious
appreciation of man, the depths of the human person are
viewed with fear and suspicion; there are protean mud flats
at the bottom of man where the flowers of evil grow. This
badness boiling up inside man separates him from God and
makes him a partner of the devil or other dark forces. This
working vision of man divides him against himself and against
God. Extrinsic religion, in other words, contributes to the
painful estrangement that modern men feel from themselves
and from God because it generates an uneasy tension in these
areas of experience. Man is a bad mixture whose nature puts
him at variance with his creator. This religious outlook on
life has thrived on fear and on the antagonism it has generated between spirit and flesh. In other words, many forms of
extrinsic religion have given man a faulty image of himself,
forcing him to feel guilty and unworthy, placing the human
condition at a great distance from God. The very thing a man
could not do and save his soul was to be himself. Life was a
battle to overwhelm the inherently bad aspects of man by
spiritual force. Unfortunately this picture of man rubbed salt
in the wounds it inflicted on man, dividing him and pulling
his personality apart. Salvation came not to unified man who
learned to live with himself but to disintegrated man who had
won the battle with himself.

It is not surprising, of course, to see the consequences of
pressing this religious template down into human personality.
Since what went on inside him was a fierce and unapproach-
able combination of lusts and meannesses, man needed constant policing. Righteousness came to the person who bent
himself to follow the laws that kept him in line. That is the
way hypocrisy was born. It is dangerous to oversimplify the
many styles of hypocrisy which have been closely associated
with extrinsic religion throughout history. It is nonetheless
clear that religious leaders have often settled for outer ob-

servance as the sign of true religious conviction. The problem
of non-integrated man, of man kept estranged by the very
force of his distorted religious commitment, was handled by
suppressive psychological techniques. These do not work very
effectively or for a very long time. When you push something
out of man's consciousness here, it pops up, perhaps in an
elaborate disguise, over there. The most obvious symptoms
of religious hypocrisy—the times when men looked good on
the surface and rationalized away their inner transgression
—were really examples of the faulty quality of this mode of
adjustment. These periods of notable hypocrisy—the high
priest in Jesus' time, the churchmen of the Renaissance, rav-
ing evangelists at almost any time—represent a breakdown in
the repressive defense system employed by extrinsic religious
forces. What was kept in the dark sprouted in strange forms,
finally making its way to the light of day in behavior
that made a mockery of the so-called religious environment
in which it flourished.

Religion that did not allow man to be himself, that did
not even allow this as a possibility, ultimately forced him into
the graceless hypocrisy that is inevitable when we do not permit things to develop according to their true nature. Hypocrisy is not just the familiar kind described above; it is not
just a world filled with Elmer Gantrys. Insofar as the forces
of extrinsic religion turned individuals away from the pursuit
of a realistic spiritual ideal, they also turned people away
from themselves. This is religious alienation in the practical
order, the switching of a person's energies toward achieving
a goal of religious behavior quite beyond and inappropriate
for him. For example, the centuries of emphasis on individual
perfection through passive acceptance of the directives of authorities gave rise to generations of Christians who were con-
vinced that their spiritual identity, the only one worth while
was determined through the judgments of persons other than
themselves. Insofar as they were encouraged to a sense of responsibility, it was to accept as wholeheartedly as possible
the plans of others for them.

This was a subtle kind of hypocrisy, not because of any
scandalous wrongdoing that lay beneath it, but because it
forced people to contradict their own honest selves, and, with

uncounted tears and sighs, to assume a pose of religious behavior that was strongly extrinsic in character. Any time you
do not allow people to be true to themselves, you are making
hypocrites of them. Worse than that, however, is the seduc-
tion of earnest people by the false images of religious perfection thereby proffered to them. The craven images that
caused men to sin were not their misshapen clay models of
divinity; misshapen models of man caused him to sin against
himself. Extrinsic religion, sensing its own powerful dynamics, allowed man only to go part of the way toward maturity;
then, with the potent offer of assured salvation for external
observance, it cut off man's growth, making comfortable room
in its pews only for those who accepted the terms it offered.

There is little wonder that men have found it difficult to
believe that it is all right to be themselves, that it is all right
for them to be different rather than all the same in their pursuit of the Spirit. The whole implication of the Incarnation
is, however, that as God became man, so man must become
man, and that this is an adult and painfully achieved destiny.
The Gospels, in other words, affirm man as an individual;
they free rather than control him; they offer a commitment to
growth rather than to magic; they sing of human possibilities
rather than of superstitious practices. Authentic religion, intrinsic faith: these invite man to personal individuation
rather than to a superficial perfection of the idealized self.

There is an attraction to the idealized notion of the self.
By this I do not refer to the healthy urge to set up a reasonable ideal and then to put one's energies into its pursuit. The
idealized self refers to a self that not only does not exist in
the present but which, because of its unrealistic quality, can
never come into being. Men have been haunted by these
phantoms throughout history, thrusting themselves forward
and breaking themselves in the effort to be something that is
truly beyond them. But the idea of this kind of ideal is indeed attractive. It supports our moments of fancy, allowing
us to identify ourselves with a heroic figure, the Walter
Mitty-like behavior of the dreamer who never comes to terms
with himself. In the Church of extrinsic religion, these ideals
have frequently had an exaggerated and misunderstood ascetic
flavor to them. This is because they are typically the kinds of

longings favored by adolescents who normally pass through a period of ascetic interest. With their energies still fresh and untapped, they may project an ideal quite unrelated to their true possibilities. It only fragments in disillusionment over the years, leaving them spent and frustrated when, for all their praying and fasting, they have not achieved the greatness of heart to which they have aspired.

There are those who believe we should have these distant ideals, even if no one ever attains them, or if they are only approached in a stumbling and painful way. Somehow, these people feel, it is good to have someone trying this hard to break the bonds that limit humanity's possibilities of growth. But, according to psychological common sense and the original feel of the Gospel, it is never a good idea to have people trying to be something they cannot be. Perhaps the most obvious example of this in the Catholic Church is the way in which celibacy has been proposed as an ideal over the years. It is normally proposed during a period in which a young person has not yet achieved his identity and during which the romance of the ideal is almost irresistible. Young people, in the phrase of Eric Erikson, overcommit themselves because they truly do not understand their own needs, their own gifts, or the real dimensions of growth which are possible for their own personalities. They do not, most of them, know themselves well enough to commit themselves to a mode of life which, because of its overinstitutionalization, forces compromises of growth on them in place of offering them real development. The Church has roughly the same track record in any ideal that it has proposed that touches on human sexuality. Enough has been written about these false ideals. We have not, however, taken a close enough look at the painful living consequences for those persons who have, with all the good will in the world, tried to be something that was really beyond them.

That is why the Church, over the centuries, came to accept bizarre adjustment rather than healthy deviation from impossible ideals. The important thing, quite consistent with the outlook of extrinsic religion, became the form, the outer surface; if this was preserved, no matter what problems were involved, all was well. But not all was well. For those persons, broken by their efforts to be something beyond themselves, ended up as alcoholics, eccentrics, or with serious psychological problems. Far worse, perhaps, were the many who ended up without ever really having tasted life at all. This was because the false ideal which they tried to give themselves allowed them neither the time nor the opportunity to discover and live in accord with their true personalities.

The grace of God, however, does not restrict us emotionally or intellectually. It does not ask us to mutilate ourselves psychologically or tell us that life is something from which we must hold ourselves back. The worst temptation of extrinsic religion is that which says we should deny the world and abstain from relating to it and its problems, that we should stand in judgment over it rather than beside it as it struggles to understand and develop itself. What, then, is the positive side of the Gospel ethic about being ourselves? If we can put aside for the moment the almost too painful realities of all the persons who have been wounded in their search for an idealized spiritual self, we still must confront the constructive aspects of the challenge to growth that is implicit in being oneself. What, in other words, can you do positively both to eliminate the obstacles to and to achieve the goal of true self-revelation?

The first thing we must be sure of is the human model we are holding up for ourselves. To put it simply, we must face what it means to be a man and put aside any dreams that would have us try to be angels or, through some other transformation, to be free from the demands of the human condition. We begin by realizing that we are complex, capable of continually surprising even ourselves, and that growth is the essential aspect of our Christian and human vocation.

We have to break through the cultural inheritance which makes us look on ourselves as if we were divided. We must break the categories that bracketed us as mind and body or flesh and spirit. It is only as we try to extend our experience of our unified selves that we will emerge from the shadow of this old prejudice and find ourselves, almost despite ourselves, as unified human beings. We cannot be afraid, then, of our feelings. They put us in contact with the depths of our experience and enable us to sense the fullness of our personalities in a manner for which there is no adequate substitute. This is the human way to sense the true measure of our own individuality. If we only think about ourselves we will never reach a thorough human appreciation of ourselves and will be limited in the manner in which we can truly express ourselves. The Spirit does not supply growth mysteriously for those who are too timid to listen to their own highly informative feelings.

We must realize without being upset by it that we are caught in the tension of being individuals while at the same time we are called to participate in shared life through some kind of community experience. Man does not survive alone, and his true self is expressed only in his relationships. This is a very broad area, including everything from the husbands and wives, their relationships with their children, and even those relationships we may have at work or at play. Tension endures because, no matter how long we live, we will always actively be involved in the process of relating effectively with others. The modern world is full of caricatures of human relationships, silly things which make this important business seem somewhat superficial. But man discovers himself in his relationship; nothing else, no matter what level of nature or super nature is invoked, makes up for it. Christ himself discovered his human identity through his experience of relationship with his parents and the other Jewish people of his time.

We are all social products. We find our real selves, not in the isolated moments when we are out of the battle of life for a moment, but in the cross-sectional view we get of ourselves in the midst of the difficulties of human relationships. There is, after all, nothing more complicated than human relationships. We can fake them, making a mask of ourselves but withdrawing at a safe distance from them, or we can take them seriously and try to make ourselves as fully present to others as we can. This is a deep and intense kind of living, the kind of living touched by the Spirit; that kind of life which is always expanding, the closest thing we know to the life to the full spoken of in the Gospels. To continue to make ourselves present to others requires a possession of ourselves and a sensitivity to our own complexity that all too few peo ple work to develop. Our real personalities are revealed in those moments when we can see just how much of ourselves we give to human relationships. In those heightened moments, perhaps in times of anger or sorrow, we get a good look at our real selves. What are we like in those moments when we have no distractions to turn us away from ourselves? In such moments we can see and hear what we are really like.

A man must also be determined not to turn away from or be disdainful of any aspects of his human experience. Whether it is in his relationships with others, or in his fantasies or idle moments, he must be ready to travel to the far edges of his personal feelings. Unless he is ready to do this with some willingness to understand he will always cut himself off from what he truly is. He will substitute another player for himself in the contest of life. This substitute in the numberless jersey may sit on the bench, never getting hurt, but never feeling alive either.

Persons are continually in process, a crooked and halting process at times, but one that is furthered by opening the self steadily to life's successive challenges. These vary, of course, with a person's age and occupation but they are always there and, despite the differences, there are common human threads which draw them together. These common features are the ground of man's experience of life in Christ. Men cannot grow, they cannot become themselves unless they are involved in some way in the rhythm of Christ's own life. That is to say, we come fully alive, whether we have heard of Christ or not, when we actively enter into the process of becoming deeply ourselves. It's in growing that we are in touch with Christ. Growth leads us, not to orgies or ecstatic trips, but to a confrontation with the gristle of the personality. We find the big obstacles to growth within ourselves. These must be acknowledged even when we find them distasteful. Clustered together and resistant, they die hard. But they are what must die if the true richness of our personalities is to come to life. We must, in other words, be able to look at the complexity of our personalities, affirming what leads us to grow, and putting to death what impedes growth.

This is in itself a redemptive process. It doesn't take place in thought or in church. This sometimes unrecognized experience of redemption takes place between ourselves and others. Transformation in Christ occurs in the growth struggles to become ourselves. For this process demands that we experience redemption in a personal manner. We must empty ourselves of what keeps us from being free and therefore from what keeps us from being human. This steady emptying of ourselves makes room for the action of the Spirit in assisting us to fulfill the promise of our personalities. This is the core of intrinsic religious experience, the fundamental initiation into and continuation of our lives caught up in Christ. Through this process we learn that being ourselves is not a lot of settling for our shortcomings but rather a continual involvement in the redemptive dying that leads to the resurrection of what we truly can be.

In other words, the determination to be ourselves is an essential condition for living in Christ. This is the very opposite of seeking to implement an ill-fitting and irrelevant self-ideal. The only thing that can be touched deeply by the Spirit is what is real; everything else falls apart under the pressure of the Spirit. The only clear road to life according to the Gospels passes through the geography of our own personalities. The only genuine religious experience is rooted in the genuine self. That is why salvation is proclaimed for everyone and why God's grace is available to any person who is honestly seeking out his own truth.

4. DO WE BELIEVE IN GROWTH?

One of the fundamental difficulties the Catholic Church has experienced during the years of renewal lies in readjusting itself to the idea that persons achieve perfection through growth rather than through sudden and dramatic jumps or transformations in their personalities. This is not to rule out those singular and seemingly instantaneous conversions which crowd the history of religious experience. These were probably far more subtly and extensively prepared for on an unconscious level than we are able fully to judge at this time. *Metanoia*, a striking Gospel theme, may not refer to an abrupt abandonment of worldly goals. This "change of heart" has often been described as an orienting of a man to God and away from what a certain school of spiritual writers lumped together as "creatures." Metanoia, looked at from the full Gospel perspective, is better than that. It describes the person who turns away from the pursuit of a false self and toward the achievement of his true personality. In other words, conversion refers to a shift of direction that does not separate a man from this world but causes him to enter more deeply and more seriously into it. Far from fleeing creatures, he begins now to see them in a new light and to place himself in relationship to them in a more open and loving way. No genuine religious conversion would make a man turn his back to the world in favor of God alone. The "changing of the weather" of a man's heart, as Dylan Thomas phrased it, indicates a new commitment to the profoundly human pursuit of life and love, to the breaking out of the self that is the beginning of the life of the Spirit. Metanoia is a word for wholehearted growth.

This change involves a man in a continuing journey. He is not, despite the scriptural twinkling of an eye, immediately a full and loving individual breathing peace and joy on his comrades. The person who sets his sights anew on becoming his true self finds that, despite the circumstances in which the intuition of grace comes to him—whether at a retreat, a *cursillo*, or on the occasion of falling in love—he is at the beginning of something rather than at the end of something. And that something is growth, the process phenomenon from which no one is exempt, that normal condition through which personalities unfold and the grace of God operates. The Spirit operates on us as we are; indeed, the Sacraments, rooted in fundamental human experiences, give clear evidence of the Church's original feeling for the way man makes his way through life. It is this sense of man as a growing individual that we somehow or other lost and are only now recovering. It is all well and good to speak of the slow wonder of human growth, but we must really ask whether we believe in it or not.

This is a deceptively simple question to which most of us, especially if we rank ourselves somewhere on the progressive side of things in the Church, would quickly give assent. But it is relatively easy to agree to the notion of growth; it only gets difficult when we take it seriously both for ourselves and for the people around us. To appreciate and respect growth is a much different thing than to sing its praises. Indeed, our practical attitude toward growth may well be a sign of whether our faith is extrinsic or intrinsic. Our convictions about growth reveal our stance toward man and determine to a large extent whether we will be able to help him grow or not. In other words, our beliefs about the way man develops have wide-ranging implications for our own style of religious faith and for the mode of religious life which we allow for others. The question of whether we are more than notionally committed to the idea of growth also has implications for our attitudes and actions toward culture and man's historical destiny.

It is easy to see that there have been times, especially during the post-Tridentine era, when the human person suffered a kind of exile from the Church. The appreciation of man as a growing individual is hard to find in the various promotions of a perfection that was largely accomplished through the careful regulation of external behavior. This model of perfection, as has been noted by so many and personally experienced by even more, has collapsed because a healthy human wisdom finds it meaningless in comparison to the true experience of growth from within. The mentality does not vanish so easily, however, or there would not be so much uneasiness in the Church about the fact that many people are obviously growing toward a more adult faith and toward a fuller personality at the same time. Growth, when it is solid and secure, should never be the source of such enduring or seemingly alarmed anxiety. That kind of worry, the kind that breeds the response of getting things back under control again, reveals clearly that some churchmen either do not value sufficiently or are not themselves mature enough to tolerate growth.

Karen Horney, the late psychoanalyst, raised important questions about our attitudes toward growth (*Neurosis and Human Growth*, Norton, 1950) and their moral implications. Noting that it would be "hazardous, indeed ruinous, to man's social and moral life" to ignore the need to pursue perfection, she points out how our answer about how man seeks his fullness depends on our views of human nature. We may, for example, cling to the belief that man is sinful, driven in some way by devil drives. We really do not even think much about the growth of man when we look at him this way. We are rather concerned with taming him, or, as Horney says, with the "overcoming of the *status naturae* and not its development" (p. 14). That vision of man leaves little room for anything but checks and restraints. Indeed, religion has expressed itself this way in the lives of countless thousands of people. This style of religion with its clear moral precepts and its available punishments for the transgressor that "keeps them in line" has had a long run in history. This very undeveloped notion of what religion is all about is clearly related to an undeveloped notion of what man is all about. The two go hand in hand. You just do not talk about growth when you must keep a wary eye on man. This keep-him-under-control image of man may have been helpful in dealing with bands of murderous Visigoths, but it surely does not fit the needs of civilized man. It cramps him and forces him to sell his own possibilities out in view of a later and greater reward. It is not, then, surprising to find a great deal of childish faith in people who have been educated to this idea of themselves by religious leaders who have such a dim view of man.

There is another version of man as well. This is not quite so absolute in its distrust of him, and yet it is not truly open to his growth possibilities either. There is something good and something bad about man. Here, as Horney notes, "the emphasis is not exclusively upon combating and suppressing evil, since there is also a positive program. Yet the positive program rests either on supernatural aids of some sort or upon a strenuous ideal of reason or will, which in itself suggests the use of prohibitive and checking inner dictates." This, after all, does not seem too unreasonable to us. It has a familiar ring to anyone strongly trained not to trust in his own powers, and to look for help to God. The problem is not, of course, that God's help is included but that here again the notion of human growth is scanted. Whatever is made up for in man is not through the expansion of some inner possibilities; it is through help from another source, from the grace of God, or from some external system of training. But that makes religion a matter of externals too, even though God is one of them. It does no disservice to God, or to traditional piety even, to realize that something is missing here as well. Respect for the human person as God created him is absent when you put aside the possibilities of growth in favor of shaping the person from the outside. This attitude has far more in common with modern-day behavior therapy than it does with the Gospel vision of man. God does not, however, work outside the normal patterns of human growth.

The Gospel vision comes far closer to the appreciation of man as having been created to grow, to master himself and his environment, and to transform both through his cooperation with the Spirit. This is not just a Rotarian or a Nixonian view of man. It quite clearly allows for obstacles that must be overcome; it sees life, in a way, as the process of dealing with the obstacles of growth. As Horney puts it:

> This belief does not mean that man is essentially good—which would presuppose a given knowledge of what is good or bad. It means that man, by his very nature of his own accord, strives toward self-realization, and that his set of values evolves from such striving. Apparently he cannot, for example, develop his full human potentialities unless he is truthful to himself; unless he is active and productive; unless he relates himself to others in the spirit of mutuality. Apparently he cannot grow if he indulges in a "dark idolatry of self" (Shelley) and consistently attributes all his shortcomings to the deficiencies of others. He can grow, in the true sense, only if he assumes responsibility for himself (p. 15).

Here, then, is a model of man that allows for his failures but sees these, along with his possibilities, as linked to the over-all process of growth. This is quite a different view of man for religion to assume, because it challenges religious figures to join in man's struggle to become himself. They must put aside the power that they formerly exercised as a means to supervise what they conceived of as man's moral behavior. It summons up a trusting and confident response, a having-faith-in man, a hoping-for man, that is not blind to man's wounds but understands that true healing comes from the inside. This is, in fact, the view of man that is consonant with an internalized religious faith, a belief system that serves as a source of integration for man's drives to grow. In any case, although this picture of man is becoming increasingly popular in the renewed Church, it is much easier to applaud it than to incorporate it as your own working model of mankind.

I know many liberally identified churchmen who are, in their relations with real people, as autocratic as a Prussian seminary rector. They still tell people how they should be, they still make demands on others that rob them of their real freedom. It is, after all, so much easier to know the way to perfection, even the new liberal superhighway, and to insist that everyone take the same route. There can be intolerance in the most avowed progressive, just as, at times, one finds a deep and redeeming vein of human understanding in an old-style churchman. That may be because there is a certain amount of experience in life that is required before we really know what we believe about other persons. And the man who has weathered a lot of life with even a small measure of openness comes to realize that you cannot force persons to grow in a certain manner, and that, if you are wise, you can only help them to find and become themselves. Almost everybody would like to think that they are truly respectful of the inner growth of others; it is an attractive ideal. We would vote for it every time. It is tested, however, in how we place ourselves in relation to them. This tells us, if we are ready to take a good look, far more about ourselves than many a dry examination of conscience. It also tells us whether we believe in the future of man in general, whether we believe that it is through man that the Spirit renews the firmament, whether we believe that man can grow wiser and more mature.

An optimistic endorsement of man's possibilities is possible for the Christian although it is almost unheard of in any other world view. That is because the Gospels urge us to affirm man and his life, to enlarge it, and to open up the horizons to which we can be guided by the Spirit. But the Spirit is made well nigh unavailable when we operate toward man as though he were a dangerous felon about to escape down some dark alley of history. The test, when we come down to it, is extremely practical. We take it every time we deal closely enough with another human being to have a real exchange with him. We cannot help but reveal whether we look on him as full of promise or full of menace. In fact, it is in putting into practice our convictions about man that we find ourselves caught up again in the redemptive dynamics that are the signs of our life in Christ. These dynamics reassert themselves at all the key points in life. We experience the meaning of life in Christ whenever we have to let our real selves out in meeting and being with others in a serious way. That is just another way of saying that, unless we pass everyone in life like the ships made formless by the night, we must put our beliefs about man on the line. If we are to make a humanly significant difference, even a small one, to others, then we have to reveal what we genuinely feel about other people. This need not be a big moment, only a real one. Whenever it is real, that is, each time we get beneath the superficial flow of life and meet the other as he or she is, then we are engaged in redemptive work. Moderns are frequently bored because their lives are so unreal and, therefore, so unredemptive for themselves or anyone else. But the person who is alive to himself and to others and who tries to respond as humanly as possible enters into the mystery of the Christian life. The proverbial way to salvation may be thought of as narrow, not to make it so exclusive as much as to emphasize that we do not travel it in anonymous saved crowds but as friends who save each other by really finding each other along the way.

The pattern is the same wherever and whenever this kind of human situation arises. We take on the flesh of our own human condition, that is, we make ourselves personally present to the other. That is what the theological notion of incarnation looks like. That is what this mytho-poetic concept comes down to. It can be as simple as a greeting that is shorn of pretense, the attention we give our child that lets him know, without undue show, that we are listening to him, the silent presence while another tells us of his troubles. This moment of engagement with the other is a barometer of our own outlook, of whether we take others seriously, whether we think we have to save them, or whether we believe in them as persons. There really is no call for anyone to get self-conscious about this. Acting concerned does not help. We always let our real selves out; we simply cannot help it, and, even if we try to wear some other mask, we still reveal the truth. There is nothing worse than fake attention or pseudo-concern anyway. Nothing is less redemptive than artifice in human relations.

The initiation of relationships leads beyond the moment of first true presence to the dynamic of death to ourselves. This is not always very dramatic either, although there can be times when the price of letting another grow can be very wrenching. This is the kind of death to ourselves that occurs if we sincerely are committed to the growth of others. We die whenever we must extend our attention when we could be off in our own bemused isolation; we die whenever we make the effort to hear the other even when we are sure that we have heard it all before. We put something to death in us when we shake ourselves loose from our own concerns in order to make room for the other in a truly human way in our lives. Some people never do this, or do it with an exasperated reluctance that shows that they have not been able to free themselves from their own selves. The important point is that no relationship in life—be it between husband and wife, teacher and pupil, or just old friends—exists in a vacuum. Each relationship is part of a whole, each one makes clear in a slightly different manner the kind of person he is and the values by which he lives. And not one of them is independent of the sustaining power of Christ's death and resurrection. For it is in what we are with each other that we experience and manifest this power. So the dying that goes into everyday living is, in large part, interwoven with our human relationships, our convictions about persons, and our willingness to put our convictions into practice. The greatest pious-sounding heresy of the century continues to be uttered by churchmen who speak of activity that is "merely human." They just don't understand how human life in Christ really is.

The cycle of recurring redemptive experience is closed by the reality of resurrection, the new life that comes to others when we have died, even in small ways, to ourselves in order to reach them. There is new life as well for the one who lets obstacles die in himself so that he can be really present with others. He is enlarged by this redemptive involvement, this risky lowering of the drawbridge of personality to allow another to cross over and be with him. It is through these kinds of experiences that we grow and give growth to others. They are fundamental to the life of the Spirit, the microcosmic presentation of the way a man who believes in growth lives his whole life with others. Mistrust has no place in this experience; neither can there be the subtle efforts at control that are so much a part of some extrinsic religion. Maneuvering is replaced by the openness to others which allows them the space to experience through us a greater sense of themselves.

We can see, in these few examples, the quality of human experience which is conducive to growth and which allows persons to be free to find the truth about themselves and to implement it in depth in their lives. Persons begin to face the obstacles to their own growth, the forces that could turn them to the pursuit of a false self, and overcome them, not so much by a life and death battle for control as by outgrowing them. That is what personal maturation is all about, and it never takes place independent of the meaning of Christ's life and death. Indeed, it reproduces and is illumined by the pervasive reality of our life in Christ.

That is the beginning of living by the Gospels, this test of whether we believe in growth or not. We do not automatically stake a claim to this merely because we have the right buttons on our lapels and the right posters on our walls. Before we move very far toward being ourselves or helping others to be themselves, we must see whether our convictions are substantial or not. The Christian life is a lot more challenging than just asking whether we believe in God or not; it asks also whether we believe in man and the power of the Spirit to release and fulfill his growth.

5. WHAT CAN WE BELIEVE IN ABOUT OURSELVES?

This is a very practical question both for individual men and for man in general. If the person himself cannot rely on or trust something in his own make-up, then he can only be cynical about his future. If men in general cannot discover something in common about their humanity which will enable them to begin to recognize and trust each other in a more wholehearted way, then the world's dream of a slowly self-realizing community is an impossible one. The Gospels are good news because they answer the question about what we can believe in about ourselves.

The false myths of history have frequently obscured any clear view of what man can believe in about himself. In the web of many inadequate but powerful myths man is the plaything of the gods, the blinded evolutionary sport of nature, or a dark-hearted but bright animal rooting around in the wastes of history only for the things that serve his own interests. The truth, which is a better name for a good Christian myth, cuts across all these notions and draws man back to a more penetrating understanding of himself. The Gospels tell us something durable about the human person, something that will outlast the false images that have interfered with man's growth throughout history.

The Christian truth, captured in the Gospels, does not make the sun into a god, or place the fate of man in control of nature's forces. Good Christian myths never succumb to such obvious strategies. That is what is remarkable about them. They do not give a magical interpretation to the universe, as understandable as that may have been to the dweller of the Andes, shivering in the shade and longing for the rise of the god-like sun that warmed him and seemed to give him life. The Christian view of man is insightful enough to look beyond this obvious method of enthroning the Sun God. It does not focus on the environment for an interpretation of man. Christian truth leads man back to himself, to the rediscovery of his own powers and his own possibilities. There is something subtle but substantial in this consistent process which has always made the person the center of life's concerns and has insisted on his maturity, freedom, and sense of responsibility. Only the Gospels have underscored the creative power of love and located its origin within man himself instead of in some magic outside of him. Man as he is co-operates with the Spirit, not to undergo some plastic surgery of the soul, but to set free the human powers of growth. Christianity is always aimed at helping man to find what he can believe in about himself.

That is why Christianity has always been described as radical. Unfortunately, in our day radical Christianity is interpreted as that style of belief which bids that men always go out to the far reaches of things in order to practice their faith. There may be need, of course, for dramatic signs of commitment to the Gospels; these are not necessary, however, for the development of intrinsic faith in the average person. Christianity is radical because it leads man back to their roots; it takes man into the depth of his personality to discover and confront himself and his challenge to grow to his own fullness. The genius of the Gospel message lies in its insistence that man must grow deeper if he is to grow larger, that man must first come to terms with the truth of himself if he is truly to live out his vocation of becoming himself. In other words, man is asked to hack himself free from the false mythologies which look to what is outside of him to explain his life and destiny. The truth lies within his personality. This process of demythologizing the gods of fate and nature is somewhat analogous to the process of psychotherapy.

We may think of the individual coming into therapy as crippled by the restrictive mythology of the false self. That is to say, the person who hurts psychologically does so precisely because he has not understood fully the truth about his own personality. He attempts to live by something that is false, by trying to fit himself into a pattern of beliefs or convictions that do not match what he is really like. This rather oversimplified summary describes the kind of mythology that powerfully controls the lives of neurotic people. They are forever blaming the world around them, their bosses, their wives, or any other incarnation of the cruel fates, for the difficulties which they encounter in life. Until they perceive the misleading nature of this mythology, they can never enter into the truth about themselves or experience what is genuine about their own personalities. Therapy becomes the process through which the individual's estrangement from his own truth is healed. He meets himself in therapy, discovering, if we stick to the language we have used earlier, the substantial myth of his own selfhood. This becomes a reliable basis for relationship to himself and to other people. He is freed through this process of self-realization to live in accord with his true personality.

This is the power the Christian Gospel message has offered to man throughout history, the strength to slash through the false myths which have prevented man from understanding and growing according to his own truth. The Gospels do not ask us to look to the stars, or to angels or miracles, but to ourselves for our salvation. They bid us to demythologize ourselves, to put aside the wispy rationalizations and half truths by which we support our own false images, and define, even at the price of considerable pain, the truth that sets us free. That is why the Gospels are about faith, hope, and love; these are the experiences that are possible for men who have learned that there is something trustworthy in their own personalities. The Gospels contain a radical message because they point to the fact that responsibility is only exercised by those who look deeply into themselves for the truth which is the only reliable basis for life in the Spirit. Willing and knowledgeable dishonesty about the self constitutes the most destructive force in human experience.

The process of discovering the truth about ourselves is not, however, analogous to unearthing a pure vein of gold behind the rocks of our unknowing. To recognize that there is something worth while in man, something that can be trusted, a reliable personal center of gravity, is not the same as saying that man is all good, true, or beautiful. Indeed, man is a mixture; there is nothing automatically absolutely good or bad about him, although the worst of the world's heresies have claimed one or the other of these distinctions for him. It is certainly possible to make a case that man is more skilled at fooling himself than at practically anything else, that he is supremely good at putting his bad foot forward. That, however, is as distorted a portrait of man as the other mythical picture of him as an innocent child of nature beneath the scars inflicted on him by civilization. Actually, man is born with the possibilities of growing, possibilities that can be denied him or diminished for him by the circumstances of his life. There is something reliable in man but it does not grow unaided or without struggle. With a destiny of growth, and a genuine capability for it, the person must work at it. That is one of the basic truths or mythic realities preserved by the Gospel: man can move forward despite the fact that he is not completely perfect. That is the nature of a growing entity. It is always incomplete, always reaching for its fullness, and always vulnerable to failure. This captures some of the essential qualities of living which, for man, is neither effortless nor hopeless. The Spirit is available to men who work at finding their own truths so that they can become fully themselves. It is denied to those men who choose the darkness rather than light, to those who reject the possibility of their own growth and settle for something less than this. It is also difficult for persons who have been hurt so much by life that they cannot find the complete truth about themselves.

The question centers on what we can believe in about man and, if this is true, how man can seem at times to be unreliable or incapable of growth. What, in other words, can go wrong, even when we recognize what is essentially positive about man? A close inspection of the person reveals a truth about the human condition which must be accepted and embraced before there can be any conception of the Christian life at all. Man is imperfect, he does bear scars, and growth is a task for which his commitment may weaken. Man does not grow automatically; he needs favorable conditions in his human environment in order to approach, understand, and love himself maturely. You can almost sense in man's difficult struggles to persevere in growth, and to pursue the truth, some kind of angry gash in his personality that is slow to heal. Continuing growth makes man more keenly aware at every step of the tension that is involved in forward movement. Everybody experiences this pain of growth, of leaving familiar things behind in order to enter the future, of giving up dependency in order to assume responsibility, of giving up security in order to achieve a new fullness of being. That this very dynamic struggle is even engaged in is one of the signals that has made many observers of man posit an internal directional force to explain the fact that man grows at all.

This inner dynamism has been given various names through the course of history. Men are, in our own age, struggling to understand it anew and to create the conditions in which man can best fill out the framework of his personality. Man is recognized as not completely divided, not totally estranged from himself; that would make his possibilities merely wishes that he could never fulfill at all. Man is rather seen in the grip of the stress of growth, more in the way in which Hippocrates spoke of disease more than twenty centuries ago. He wrote of the fact that every illness had an element of suffering, the *pathos* that is so easy to recognize and which some might mistakenly identify as illness itself. There is another element, however, the *ponos* or toil, the work of health, the struggle sparked by the vital forces by which man constantly attempts to heal and put himself together again. This is what man is like, not just a victim at the mercy of good or bad fortune, but as a locus of power from within himself which he can muster up in order to continue the process of his own healing and growth in his experience of life.

Harry Stack Sullivan, the famous psychiatrist, wrote that the "basic direction of the organism is forward," an opinion seconded by psychoanalyst Karen Horney, who said that "the ultimate driving force is the person's unrelenting will to come to grips with himself, a wish to grow and to leave nothing untouched that prevents growth." This is re-emphasized in the special language used by many other careful students of man. There is just something about him, complex and painful though it may be to understand, that motivates man to come to grips with himself and to try to do right by himself. There is, in other words, something that you can believe in about man, an inner but not an alien force, the inborn aptitude for positive growth. This kind of growth is not an easy thing, either to experience or to appreciate. It is seeded with complications and it is never completely over and done with. This is, however, the power in which we must believe or we are forced into one of two positions. First, we may believe that man has no chance at all because he is powerless of himself to influence his destiny and so will eventually destroy himself. On the other hand, if we do not accept a positive core in man, we must suppose that God makes up for everything that man lacks, that God does not operate on man as human, but man the puppet, whose powers of movement come from above.

We may have to meditate on man and his works, or think deeply about ourselves and the course of our own lives, to become aware of the fact that God does make us to grow, that we can assume a considerable measure of responsibility for this, and that a prime obligation of our lives is to love ourselves enough to see that we fulfill ourselves. Notions of self-fulfillment are redolent with connotations of superficial and self-satisfying flights of fancy: a little dabbling here, then a little further interest in something there for self-amusement in the name of self-fulfillment. This is far from understanding the meaning of true self-realization, and it is a long distance away from comprehending with any kind of understanding the growth possibilities which we all possess. If we believe that we can grow, then we must take ourselves, and the lives of those around us, seriously. The pursuit of ourselves is not a duty, but a privilege, a way of fulfilling our calling to nothing less than fullness of life for ourselves and those whose lives are touched by our own. The passage of life is forward. Man moves to make more out of himself; he does not stand still.

We come to terms, at this point in our reflections, with our first real grasp of the meaning of the faith that is preached to us in the Gospels. Faith, for many people, is a luminous but insubstantial thing, a sometime gift that supports belief in things beyond ourselves. Faith, for many, is something like agreeing to believe in the impossible. This, however, is the kind of faith that smacks of magic, the pie-in-the-sky kind of promises that are really unrelated to the day-to-day experience of life itself. Faith, in this view, is another realm from the human. The Gospels tell us, however, that faith that does not begin with a commitment to the human is no faith at all.

The first commitment in faith is to the possibilities of man. What we believe in, what we count on in any aspect of human life, is the inner force that is freed by the Spirit to move man in the direction of greater growth. Faith does not ask us to believe in the impossible. It asks us rather to believe in what is possible for us. That is to say, faith cannot be factored out from the human condition, or removed from this root business of facing and becoming ourselves. Our faith, in the operational Christian life, rests not in the clouds but in ourselves and in all our brothers in the human condition.

Faith invites us to look beneath the different colors, the different customs, even the catalogue of horrors that you can find without looking very hard in history, to see man's possibilities beneath it all. If man is to have a future that is not going to be controlled by those who would condition him or manipulate him through some other means, then it will be made available to him by those who continue to believe in him and to realize that the phrase "merely human" does not have any real meaning in the Christian view of the world. Faith enables us to see man in the true dimensions of his life. Faith does not merely say that man has a miserable and strenuous life below which will be made up for by a life later on. Faith makes a connection between these two, showing that the beginnings of growth are here and now. For those touched by the Spirit death is not something absolutely new, or something dreadfully strange. It is, in fact, the transforming step that takes man to the true identity of his full growth.

If man is not able to believe in himself, then he can only project, like searchlights against the sky, his inner longings for fullness on the sun, the moon, and the stars, to all of which he has entrusted his destiny at different times in history. The Gospels say that belief begins in looking into oneself, in learning to live without the support of our false myth-symptoms that take the responsibility away from us while they cripple our growth at the same time. Faith is not so mysterious after all. It is an essential condition for a healthy Christian life, the laying open of man to himself and to others which is fundamental to any growth toward human individuality or human community. There are examples of this kind of faith all around us in life all the time. The unfortunate distortions of the Christian message over the last centuries have made us look for something outside of man's ordinary life, supernatural subtitles, which are really the explanation of the Christian life. You cannot accurately call any experience of faith by the slightly degrading names of "natural faith" or "merely human." This kind of language reflects a foreshortening of faith, a restricted view of reality which makes the man who uses these phrases search the sky and miss the meaning of man in the process.

For example, this fundamental faith in man is clearly perceived whenever a man seeks to discover and deal with his own truth. He is getting at himself, wiping away the grime and clearing away the obstacles which have made it hard for him to find himself. He is beginning, in other words, to count on himself, and to uncover the God-given core of his own personality. We see this kind of faith whenever a man and a woman commit themselves to each other in the great, utterly simple mystery of drawing goodness and greatness out of each other through a life of growth together. A man and woman have faith in each other, not because they think they are completely perfect in that instant, but because they truly believe in the possibilities of one another. They know, in other words, that they can rely on something lasting in each other. This is the kind of vision that true faith enables us to have. It generates the kind of hope that enables people to reach out to each other throughout a lifetime, and to give each other the courage to continue growing when this seems the weightiest and the most difficult of life's challenges. It is this kind of faith that enables man to break through the icy covering of narcissism, to break free of the restricted preoccupation with his own superficial self, and to see for the first time his own individuality and his necessary connection and urgent vocation to respond to others. Faith is the beginning of our response to others, the substantial root of our response, as Eliade notes, to the other who is God.

The false mythologies about man cover him the way wild vines obscure a house. They must be torn away if we are ever to get an understanding of the structure beneath. Sometimes it seems that ripping this growth away will be too painful, perhaps even too destructive for the dwelling that is shrouded by such foliage. We can have the same feelings about ridding ourselves of the burdensome mythologies that have made us look in every direction but the right one to understand the meaning of Gospel faith and the life of the Spirit. These false mythologies are wicked not because they offend God, but because they offend man. They are sinful because they offer a distorted model of life for man, saying that he must force himself into it in order to find salvation. He has tried to do this over the centuries but he has always crippled himself in the process. Renewal in the Church is really a time in which man is healing himself of the effects of these previous experiences and attempting to walk again under his own direction and with his own strength. For example, there is the myth, which dies very hard, that man must always limp through life because there is something permanently wrong with him. This is a myth that does not respect man's potential. It tends to make him passive and unable to help himself; it makes it difficult for him to open himself to the power of the Spirit because it plagues him with feelings of unworthiness. Then there is the myth that all of man's struggles are only human, found at a cheap cut-rate level of life, struggles whose "naturalness" must be made up for by a power that operates independently of and without any direct relationship to the human person. A related myth says that there is some kind of magic outside of us, by whatever name we call it, that substitutes for the living process of achieving growth. There are, however, no skipped steps in man's way to his own fullness. Not even God does that to man; he respects his capacity to walk and he lets him make his way a step at a time.

On the other hand, as was mentioned earlier, there are dangerous mythologies which in an utterly naïve way expect that man is totally good, capable of an innocent unfolding to perfection without any hard lessons in self-knowledge, conflict with others, or painful growth involved. This is as cruelly deceptive as the notions which put all the emphasis on the power of God to make up for fragile man. History has had recurrent periods of infatuation with the myth of the child of nature, the eternal dream that growth comes out of the very pores of people, and that a new and blessed generation will save us all. That is the force that is supposed to green Reich's America. He speaks of hopes, but he does not give much evidence of understanding the way man grows. Reich does not realize that no man achieves his destiny aside from living in the mystery of Christ. As long as man gives in relationship to the transforming reality of Jesus' presence, then the way will not be smooth. What faith in man says is that it will be possible. It will not be effortless. It will depend on involvement in the life, death, and resurrection rhythm that is the pulse of all life.

Other and professionally more dangerous mythologies are on the horizon. There is, for example, the notion that man's future can be planned out by technicians, a new world fashioned by the antiseptic engineers who have made themselves into a new priesthood to minister to the destiny of man. We need a healthy skepticism about the philosophies of physicists and engineers, biologists and aerospace equipment designers, the kind of men speaking freely now about genetic control, the licensing of those who bear children, and a hundred other precision-honed visions of life in the year 2000. It takes a wisdom beyond most of these scientists to engineer a life style that will truly allow man to grow. They have not mastered the design of freeway entrance and exit ramps yet; it is hard to entrust the future environment of the human person to them.

If we are committed to the notion that human beings can grow, then we must take man more seriously. We must broaden Pope Paul VI's plea that every sexual act must be open to life. This is hardly an adequate Christian vision of the setting in which man can move, from the base of strength given to him by God toward the fullness of life to which he is called. We must make it possible that every human action and circumstance is open to life. Our duty is to see that man has an opportunity to live as man and that he be freed of the mythologies heaped on him by those who think that he is wicked as well as by those who think that he is supremely innocent. We must make it possible for man to see himself as he is, a dynamic unity who moves in the right direction if he is given the right opportunity and encouragement to do so. The Church's business is not merely to proclaim faith in another world; it is to make an act of faith in this one. The Gospels say that man can count on himself, that he can reach himself and others through the power of Christ's redeeming life. That power of the Spirit is available to him, not to replace his efforts to live, but to make it possible for him to live fully.

6. HOW CAN IT ALL GO WRONG?

If there is something positive in man, how can he end up living very negatively; if he is born to grow, how can he settle for being a cripple? These are difficult questions, challenging us to inspect the dark side of man whose shadows seem to validate Freud's notion of a death instinct. We are familiar with man's raping and killing, his spoiling of civilization. Man can be a barbarian but he can sometimes also seem to be not much of anything, a passive spectator of history, giving up on growth in favor of a self-defeating sense of security. Where does man step in the manhole; how is it possible for him to neglect or distort his own potential for growth?

These questions have been asked about man often enough in history. We ask them here with a special concern for the life of the Spirit. This too can get mixed up, reflecting in its fads the various images of half-grown or neurotically developed man. The fashions in spirituality have reflected the images of man held tightly if unfortunately by the churchmen who shaped or misshaped Christian personality through the ages. Christians have come to understand that the Church has, tradition and special guidance of the Spirit notwithstanding, absorbed and operated on the basis of wrong or partial ideas of man. Because of these the Church has proclaimed moral teachings that are built with everlasting shakiness on an inadequate understanding of human personality. Many of these are now questioned in the light of rediscovering a more hopeful and positive image of man. How could it be, people ask, that the Church could have incorporated so much subtle error and caused so much suffering if it did indeed have some kind of right not to be wrong in these very important matters?

One of the thorniest theological discussions, conducted, it might be noted, at a great distance from ordinary life, centers on trying to discover a way of saving the Church's face about the mistakes it has made concerning man. This is a question which rankles and disturbs persons, a question which has not had nearly enough public discussion. If, after all, the Church employed wrong ideas about man, then these notions necessarily distorted the ideas the Church had about man's righteous or sinful behavior. The problem arises, of course, because churchmen consistently invoke tradition, the notion that the Church has always taught something or taught it for such a long time, to defend against modifying moral positions which no longer seem tenable in view of our present understanding of human persons. If the Church has always been right, then it is very difficult for it to admit that it could have been wrong without forcing itself to take a close look at many other unquestioned aspects of its relationship to the human race. How could all this have happened? The question is not just how can man as an individual go along and not grow; rather, it comes to saying how come the Church, which has claimed a right to be right, has, in fact, made mistakes and failed to deepen its understanding of man?

The answer is, of course, that it was not easy for the Church, through its theologians, to make this kind of mistake. This epical crack in the columns of theological wisdom demanded that they depart notably from the image of man that we find in the Gospels, as well as from the optimistic commitment to incarnation that is at the very basis of their good news. Perhaps it is understandable, in an organization as old as the Church, that distortions could insinuate themselves gradually, and that if we had the patience and the skill, we could reconstruct these developments very clearly. It was not easy for all this to happen, but it was even harder on the individuals who have suffered because of these distorted notions. It is hard still today on persons who suffer with its own original understanding of the human person.

Perhaps we can understand how the Church lost its way in understanding man if we examine how an individual can lose his way, miss the opportunity for growth, and end up moving sideways or backwards in life. To do this we will employ the analogy of the person and the kinds of crippling problems which he experiences when the conditions for his psychological development are thwarted by certain internal or external factors. For example, an individual born with some organic psychological deficit has a limit placed on his growth which he can never fully overcome. Limited growth, of course, does not mean that no growth takes place; it does indicate the way our growth as persons is conditioned by our internal health or lack of it. Far more influential are the psychological factors which come from outside the individual. These are largely interpersonal influences, although they can be affected by severe environmental problems such as wars, depressions, or other major dislocations of the world around the growing individual. We focus here, however, on the interpersonal effects on the growth of the person of those closest to him at the crucial stages of his development. These are ordinarily the individual's parents, the persons who give him life and who are charged with enlarging his life. This is a recognizably delicate process, and the impact of the parents on development is very strong. They either open up life for the individual; or they can close it off. Parents, after all, give the individual his first sense of himself, his first primitive feeling of whether he is wanted or not, his first intuition of whether or not the world is a trustworthy place.

Parents interpret the universe to the young child. It is the mother and father who name the stars and the animals and, most important of all, the individual's first human feeling experiences. We may not think of it very often, but our ideas of what love means come from those around us, both in the way we experience it throughout our personality, and the soundness of our understanding of the word itself. Parents can, after all, insist that a child accept a symbolic word like love to explain an experience which is very distant from love. This is the kind of process which dams the river of growth, turning it aside or letting it grow stagnant. In this sensitive area immature parents can have a lasting and destructive effect on their children. Healthy people, of course, introduce their children to the world around them without much self-consciousness. They can even make many mistakes while they do it; in fact, there is no other way to raise a child except imperfectly. The parents who demand perfection in their children cause most of the difficulty for a growing child.

In the course of the ordinary individual's life, however, sincere parents who are honest with themselves and who attempt to be loving and fair with their children do most of the important things well enough to promote growth in their offspring. They help the child to develop a sense of his own worth, and an appreciation that he is good because they love him. They do not engender needless feeling of guilt as they help the growing infant to assume a sense of responsibility for his actions and for himself. He learns about love from them through the experience of their loving. He can trust the word they give him to describe the experience; it is his for life, and when he uses it the word love will have a substantial meaning. What the person learns through the many aspects of his closeness with his parents and the way his slowly enlarging vocabulary comes to express these experiences: these are converging factors that overlap each other. His idea of himself matches what he really is. This is the essential equation that is necessary for the positive growth of the individual to take place. He still will not grow without various hitches, misgivings, and misunderstandings; he will be headed in the right direction, however, because no distortions of a major kind will have been introduced into the individual's understanding of himself, his most important experiences, and the world around him.

It is very different in the case of the individual whose parents are not capable of a free and loving response to him. The distorted shape of the future person comes off the drawing board of the marriage relationship of the parents because out of this arises their relationship with their children. Enough stories have been written about the powerful quality of the parents' influence on the child. It is in the interaction of neurotic parents with children, parents who force the child to accept their version of the world and of the child's own experience, that we begin to understand how growth can be frustrated. If the growing individual does not develop a sense of basic confidence in others and in himself, then he cannot get himself together for gradual forward growth in life. The parents can manipulate the child into accepting a false image of himself—taking their interpretation that he loves, for example, when he really is confused or is angry—because they give or withhold that which the child needs most of all, their love. When they love the child only on the condition that the child respond in exactly the ways they wish, then the parents have pressured the developing personality away from seeking its own truth and toward accepting a highly distorted interpretation.

Parents do this, for example, when their needs to have the perfect child make them intolerant of his failings. I recall well an adult priest friend of mine who had attained a position of high responsibility but who in middle age was still suffering from the fact that his best was never good enough for his parents. The mark of it all was still on him: the hesitancy, the withdrawal that made him wear loneliness like a shroud, the stuffy façade that covered the person who could have been there. He was never able to find the right combination to please his parents. Although his grades were the highest in his class, his mother and father always expected more. He is still trying to please some distant father-figure in an unconscious psychological way. He has never grown beyond being the eager-to-please little boy hurrying home with gold-starred report cards to unappeasable parents. Parents make it difficult for the child to grow when they are unwilling to let the child grow to fulfill his own personality. When they insist that he be shaped according to their own desires or needs, and they do this through the manipulation of love, they make it quite literally impossible for the individual to grow in his own direction. How can man fail to grow? Man fails when those who are charged with helping him to achieve the full experience of life fail, because of their own problems, to do this.

The result of this is a negative neurotic kind of growth in which the individual seeks to fulfill an image of himself that is not at all what he is like. The neurotic confronts a hopeless quest because, not knowing his true self, he tries to plaster together a fragmented image of himself with such psychological defenses as are at hand. He bolsters himself, keeps himself together through the distorting effect of these defenses; they permit him to look on himself according to the misshapen interpretation of his experience which he started to amass early in life. This false self-concept cannot serve as the basis of true growth. The person presents himself in life through a distorted notion of himself. He always wonders why his relationships never quite work out as he had hoped, why real love is beyond his grasp, and why he finds himself so isolated and lonely. That is the penalty of neurotic growth, a style of development which can be pursued with great vigor, but with enormous effort to keep the defenses intact in order to keep the person in some kind of stable maladjustment. When anxiety breaks through the ill-fitting edges of this false image like wind through worn-out windows, the person may turn to psychotherapy to begin the laborious task of redefining himself in a more realistic way. During this time the forces for positive growth may be freed again through the personal instrumentality of the therapist whose training enables him to help the person discover his real personality and to begin to implement his possibilities.

The same kind of process holds true for the religious development of man, an aspect of personal growth which cannot really be isolated as though it were truly a separate thing. In religion, however, false images have been forced on man in great numbers. They signify an estrangement from the person we meet in the Gospel. These images have led men, at different times in history, to do the most extraordinary and inhuman things in the name of Christ. This applies to all those phenomena from energetic Christians out to kill enemies or to mutilate themselves. Something like the strange and crippling process of the parental interaction with the child must have occurred to allow men to pursue such false ideas of religious perfection. The Church has manipulated another force, almost as powerful as love—that of fear and guilt, to force men to accept its interpretation of their experience, their human potential, and the course of their lives. This has not served the integration of the individual but has, in fact, tended to break him into pieces, to cripple him so that his goals of religious behavior have been severely limited while, at the same time, dependent on the authorities of the

Church itself. Fear is here almost as influential for man as love. Fear, whether we want to admit it or not, has been expertly used throughout the years with great effect upon human beings. The fear of hell and eternal damnation has been a powerfully controlling factor which has brought control at the high price of frustrating the authentic and positive growth of the religious dimension in man's personality.

Through the manipulation of fear the following results can be seen: of all things, the use of fear has kept man from developing his religious faith as deeply as is possible. In fact, fear has kept faith on the surface of life, on the level of personal salvation above all else. Faith never develops when man is not brought to view religion in terms that go beyond his own self-concern. Manipulation and fear have restricted the range of man's view, even as the manipulation of love restricts the individual's view of his own person. In other words, the reason that religion has had such a narrow definition in life flows from its limitation to a very narrow range of behavior, not too far removed from the rituals of magic or the placating of the gods. The manipulation of fear has prevented men from integrating religious experience with the rest of life. This has prevented man from truly sensing the existence and meaning of the religious dimension of his own personality.

Manipulation and fear have fostered an exaggerated dependence on authority. This has caused people to doubt themselves, to think that they are anything but trustworthy in deciding about the probity of their own behavior or about the soundness of their own religious aspirations. In this model, everything affecting the religious dimension of life was funneled through authority. Even the image of sanctity was very carefully designed to dampen the spontaneity of life, to keep man, made for so much more in life, responsive to quick and complete control.

An appreciation of these dynamics explains why it has been so difficult for man to move forward in understanding himself or the genuinely religious aspects of his life. So many distortions have been introduced, and so many sidetracks opened up, that it is little wonder that man has had difficulty in finding the correct direction for himself. He has, in fact, pursued neurotic growth, bolstering his inaccurate ideas about faith and religion by defensive mechanisms which have actually closed him off from authentic religious truth. The forces of religious growth, in other words, can be frustrated, or turned aside, especially when ecclesiastical authority figures manipulate, to their own ends, the potent forces of guilt and fear.

Man is currently recovering his direction, sensing again within himself his potential for personal and religious growth, and realizing that these are not antagonistic but complementary aspects of himself. This reintegration enables man to put aside his defenses and to find a new and more satisfactory model for his own total personal growth. In other words, as man puts himself together, he also understands with fresh insight the religious dimension of his personality. He knows that its growth was arrested by the enormous influence of authoritarian religious figures who controlled man's religious development within the cramped space bordered by guilt and fear. Man has begun to free himself from the forces that have made it difficult for him to do anything but settle for immature faith.

How could man go wrong in this most important dimension of experience? He went wrong because men who would be gods went wrong, and tried to keep religion drawn on the reduced scale of their own immaturity. Man became alienated from his deepest religious aspirations, but, through the power of the Spirit, is now healing himself again.

7. WHERE DO WE EXPERIENCE THE SACRED?

Rightly or wrongly, most of us have been educated to find the sacred somewhere out of the course of ordinary human events. The sacred, as something set apart, has come to have an existence of its own; so we have sacred places, objects, and times, which exist next to but distant from our usual human experience. We change ourselves to some extent when we address ourselves to the sacred. We put aside the things which normally occupy us in this world in order to be concerned about something from another world.

Religious experience, as a sample of the sacred, has been edged out of ordinary life to have the same kind of separated meaning. Religion is conceived of as an experience of the transcendent, something that takes us out of time, away from the here and now, and into another dimension of existence. Unusual religious experiences, where and when they are described for us, are powerfully transforming and occasionally terrifying for the individuals who experience them. Indeed, in culture today people actively seek experience which will remove them from the pains and pressures, and even the boredom, of life. Drugs are employed for many reasons, not the least among them being the pursuit of religious-like experience to satisfy some of the uncharted longings of the human psyche. Some seriously promote drugs as the new world's avenue to religious experience, which seems otherwise hard to come by. This "chemical ecstasy," as it is called, supposedly offers man the controllable opportunity to feel at first hand the unsuspected wonders of the inner and outer environment.

Life for the average Christian, however, does not leave

much time even for scientific pharmaceutical journeys into the realms that have been called religious. After all the interest and analysis of the "mystical," especially at seminars of scholars who look too dried out to experience a good temptation, much less a religious ecstasy, the Christian is faced with life, homely, overwhelming, and indifferently dressed as it waits for him every morning. The fact is that the average Christian is not, and may not care to be, snatched up into the heavens; neither does he experience the darts of mystical love piercing and warming his heart. Most people just do not encounter religious experience of this transforming sort even though they may believe in it firmly. Some of them may even pray for it or long for it in the typical adolescent fantasy of leading a withdrawn and holy life. It does not, however, occur for most of the uncounted millions who are faced with the challenge of living the life of the Gospel. It never has occurred in their lives and, in fact, they might begin to worry if this kind of extraordinary religious experience, whether induced by drugs or not, ever becomes the ideal. The Gospel life is just not led or rewarded that way.

The urge to suspend time and to crack the barrier of the human in order to experience a sense of unity with the divine is common enough. I am not here questioning the mystics whose religious lives have been located near the intense limits of human experience. They have spoken and written of the deep silence which they have known in the moments when they feel they have been in close contact with God. They are, however, very wordy, as the distinguished researcher Otto noted, in speaking and writing about it afterwards. (R. Otto, *The Idea of the Holy*, tr. J. W. Harvey [London: Oxford University Press, 1928], p. 2). In any case, these have always been labeled as "extraordinary" experiences in the tradition of the Church, and there is little reason to expect that they will ever become anything other than this. In the same way, we have a paucity of visions and miracles in the modern-day world. Perhaps this reflects a new attitude toward what we expect in religious experience that flows from an intrinsic kind of faith. Miracles and wonders are very supportive for an extrinsic religious faith. They are not nearly so significant for persons who have had to deal with the meaning of religion as an internalized and integrating force. Perhaps it can safely be predicted that the age of searching for a deepened faith will not witness very much in the way of extraordinary religious experiences. In fact, the most telling questions about the need for wonders come, not from the skeptics of doubting scientists, but from profound believers who do not feel that faith consists so much in the unusual, and who do not expect faith to lift them out of this world as much as to light it up for them. Internalized faith leads man to take a deeper look as he seeks an explanatory structure for life as he experiences it. He is more distracted than helped by some extraordinary and perhaps culturally related forms of religious experience. Visions seem to have flourished in countries which have always encouraged and tolerated public expression of emotional experience.

After all the wonders have dazzled the world, their real message still remains. This is a message of faith, that the work of salvation is not going to be accomplished by suspending the laws of nature around man, but by man's confrontation with his own responsibility inside himself. The message of the miracles and of the unusual lives where valid mystical experience seems to have taken place is the same. We are not adrift in the galaxies like a slowly spiraling mote in a shaft of sunlight. We are in relationship to our Creator, life does make sense, and we can be touched, strengthened, and challenged by the Spirit. For most men religious experience consists in responding to the problems of life and love in a manner that looks ordinary indeed. We are passing out of the age of wonders, but not away from the message which these have always been intended to convey. It is like passing out of the village of Lourdes, with its commercial shacks tumbling one over the other, and into the quiet grounds where one senses faith rather than spectacle as the focus of the experience.

Religious experience, the encounter with the sacred, is associated with an intensity and reality of living that is possible only to growing persons. It can occur only in this life, within the hours, days, and persons of our experience. It is not separate from life, but that does not make it any the less potent. Internalized faith is a powerfully integrating, unifying, and explaining force which enables man to see and deal with life in a perspective of Gospel values. This faith makes it possible for man to see more in his human experience; it does not tell him to look away from it in order to experience the divine. Religious experience is rooted in those aspects of life where man pursues his humanity, where, in other words, he is sensitive and open to himself and to other men and, therefore, must fully open to the supporting and enlarging power of the Spirit. Fully developing man is the most powerful sign of the Spirit's action, the clearest indication we possess of the existence of the sacred.

Man senses and energizes the religious dimension of his personality when he gives and experiences growth. This takes place when he most keenly feels and responds to his obligations to himself and to others; this is where, in other words, he can see most clearly how, as one individual, his life is immersed in the mysterious reality of existence. Here he understands that his experience as an individual, as a member of a community, and as a child of God possesses an essentially unified quality. He not only knows this intellectually but, because religious experience is a response of the total person, he may feel it throughout his being. What he understands is that these aspects of his experience—as an individual, as a community member, as a creature to his Creator—are really one. These are inseparable realities rather than layers of existence; they constitute the true world in which man lives, the geography of which is illumined by mature faith. In other words, an essential aspect of man's religious experience, or his meeting with the sacred, occurs as he realizes the truth about himself. This complex but simple truth tells him that he is not alone, that his life is not a chance accident, and that he has a right to hope in his Creator who is faithful in his promises to him.

This astounding good news is only apprehended and understood by someone who lives deeply in the here and now. This experience of the sacred comes to man, not when he tries to break the bonds of himself, but when he enters as deeply as possible into the experience of himself as a living person. The temptation of our first parents has been interpreted as that in which they aspired to be more than themselves. This temptation comes again, however, to every man invited freely to respond to his Creator. This primordial temptation endures in the subtle invitation repeated to every man, to be less than fully human, to corrupt one's freedom by neglecting it rather than by overusing it. Authentic religious experience makes a man sense throughout himself the opportunity and responsibility that his life offers to him. Man can accept it and become himself or he can turn aside, looking for life elsewhere, waiting to be transformed from outside rather than struggling to grow from within.

The pity is, of course, that men have rushed out to find wonders here and there at all kinds of time and places in history. Indeed, we have had an embarrassment of riches as far as the crisis-oriented manifestations of pseudo-religious experience are concerned. By a strange quirk that is part of the temptation not to be human, people have listened to false prophets by the vanload. This is part of the deceptive perennial promise of magic, the immature mythology that has cheated man out of becoming himself. That kind of extrinsic religious experience, manipulating salvation the way a barker manipulates the peas under the walnut shells, has arrested the religious development of man and prevented him from really entering into himself. Nothing in genuine religious experience ever turns man away from his true self; the intensity with which a man may experience his own depths can be painfully dazzling, but not because man has been thereby assigned a false identity. Genuine religious experience confirms man and his authentic struggle for personal incarnation. Religious experience validates the human in a radical way but it never denies it.

The sacred, then, is experienced at the most intense moments of human life, when man gets, at least briefly, a view of his own depths. Then, with his own genius and tools, man tries to symbolize and express this experience. He has done this through the centuries in art, music, and drama. What he has experienced in a sharply human way, he makes signs of through his startling gifts of creativity. Man makes places and creates moods to memorialize profound insight. He designs these environments, whether they are cathedrals or home liturgies, to enable him to rediscover or re-enter the religious experience in which he faced his own complete truth so deeply.

Man's signs of the sacred are not alien to life. They are rather supremely expressive of life because they are signs of faith and hope. They are carved, painted, or built in a human language which can be recognized by anyone who has fought through to an awareness of his own depths. Sacred objects and places are not superficial memorials to placate disagreeable gods in the skies. They are not deceptive and wish fulfilling scarecrows to keep the evil spirits away. The most sacred signs are the most humanizing, because they have their foundation in man's encounter with life. Churches, rites, and prayers are truly sacred when men have brought life to them. They are signs of life, of rich and deep human life, or they are not signs of anything at all. It is very hard for men otherwise to wrench life from liturgies or prayers which are not really expressive of the human person. That is why so many people have had such a frustrating experience with the liturgy. They have expected the liturgy to produce life more than symbolize life; people have demanded life of it. The liturgy becomes a truly religious experience when Christians bring life to it.

The person who opens himself to his own truth necessarily opens himself to the power of the Spirit; this profound human experience precedes the development or appreciation of sacred places. Man alive, the glory of God according to St. Irenaeus, is the only builder of the sacred. Otherwise magic and not Christian meaning inhabits the place. Man must experience a fullness of his existence in order to intuit the full dimensions of reality. Reality necessarily includes the realms, so hard to describe, in which God's powers are felt in human beings. Any explanation of sacred experience that departs from the effort to be truly human is intellectualization at best, and primitive neurotic deception at its worst.

If the sacred and the real have such a vital relationship to each other, where does man experience the sacred? If it is here and now rather than out there and later on, if it is in the order of what is usual rather than in what is extraordinary, where in our own lives do we sense the sacred? In the human exchanges which demand most of us, where we must move out of the shallows and into the depths of our personality, where we must take the risk of living rather than just avoid the possibility of failure: in all these man touches and is touched by the sacred. Whenever he enters into life at the level where he experiences himself, others, and through these a hint of the dimensions beyond the moment, man is on sacred ground. When do these kinds of experiences occur? Are we ready to recognize them as the ordinary settings for our most real experiences of life in Christ?

The sacred in our human experience always has the signs of the Gospels burned into it. There is no experience of the sacred, in other words, that allows us to look away from the fundamental linkage of incarnation, death, and resurrection. This sacred and inseparable chain is always present for the person who lives deeply by faith. There is no sacred experience that takes you completely out of this life, making it unnecessary to face existence, the suffering that it entails, or the fullness of life to which it leads for those who embrace it generously. If this fundamental sign is lacking, the sacred experience fails; it is counterfeit and insubstantial, a fashioning for lesser gods that does not bear the weight of living by the Gospels. So too, the sacred opens a person to all that faith expects of him even as it consolidates the kind of growth which faith has already achieved. The sacred stretches us to greater possibilities of growth. It never gives us an experience that ends only in itself. It breaks us out of ourselves, then, into a new awareness of the social demands of Christianity. It shatters the personal security orientation of extrinsic religious faith. The person who faces the complete truth about himself, as it can be understood only by the light of the Spirit, is a growing person, not a finished one. He is a man on pilgrimage and he manifests the signs of the Spirit's presence as he works at becoming actually himself.

Some will ask if there is not a place here for the phenomenon which is known as the gift of tongues. Is not the experience of ecstatic prayer a celebration of the sacred in our lives? This may well be so. I am not interested in making a case against those who speak in tongues. Some tongue speakers evidence the vitality of the Spirit's presence in their full

Christian lives. Others clearly reflect the somewhat shaded neurotic edge of religious practice. It does little good to make a case against the possibility of the Spirit's operating in this fashion with persons. I am not sure, however, that this highly personal kind of experience is a desirable or convincing sign of the fact that God loves the world and wants men to love one another. Insofar as the Gospel life is concerned, however, I think it is safe to say that the gift of speaking in tongues is not within the ordinary experience of the struggling Christian. We are concerned here with putting our focus on the experience of the sacred that is inevitable for anyone who truly opens himself to the problems of mature living. Perhaps tongue speaking helps some to discover more of themselves and, therefore, constitutes a rich experience of the work of the Spirit. Alas, most people simply do not have this or any other extraordinary spiritual experience in their lives. They just have life and they have to find themselves in the Spirit as best they can as they make their way through it.

Where does the average man have the chance to look deeper into himself and to sense the unity of personal and spiritual experience? Where do we look for those powerful intuitions that tell us that we are in the presence of the sacred? These are the experiences which take place, for example, when a man and woman meet each other for the first time and sense that they are going to love each other throughout a lifetime. There is a power in that moment, one that begins to transform their hearts and to steel them for their long and trying journey together. There is a sacred aspect to this initial discovery of another person whom I see as separate and distinct from me, the person who responds enough to break me out of my own narcissistic self-concern. This is a moment of incarnation, which yields in short order to the series of deaths that are built into loving as people try to give life to one another through all their days. This is a common experience, men will say, and one that can be overly romanticized so that people think they experience more than what really takes place. This is exactly why there is an element of the sacred in it. When we live truly in relationship with someone we love, we may be encouraged by the romantic experience, but we will never be able to stop short at it. There is always the challenge, the utterly realistic problem of dying and rising in a redemptive continuity of substantial love. This does not happen when something is merely romantic; it takes place only when real love is present. The signs of the redemptive cycle are clearly there.

An individual experiences the sacred when he is faithful to another person, to his given word, or to his commitment to a cause even when he feels keenly how much that demands of him. Man cannot be faithful without being more of himself. Fidelity does not come out of a personality we have safely banked; fidelity arises from our inter-relationship with the flow of life. It is something that comes out of a person who is mature enough to deepen his convictions in the moments when they are severely challenged. Fidelity, in other words, is not something that exists because we stay the same. It is a dynamic quality that exists because we are capable of creative growth and constructive change.

So too, in a reality that goes beyond the limits of humanism, a person experiences the sacred when he is true to his own best possibilities, that is, when he draws up from within himself all his potential strength and utilizes it as best he can. There is a great deal of suffering and dying involved in this process; being true to the self demands the follow-through on incarnation, death to the false self in order to achieve the fullness of resurrection.

A person experiences the sacred when, with a fully knowing and vulnerable heart, he forgives another for an injury that he has experienced from him. Confrontation with the self and dealing with the contradictory feelings which must die if this forgiveness is to be complete involve a man in the essential aspects of the redemptive process. He cannot fully forgive another without the power of the Spirit, and this is made available to him when he defeats the forces that would make him turn into himself in vindictive self-content.

An individual experiences the sacred when he stands with and works through a difficult life experience with another person. This can occur between husband and wife in times of misunderstanding, disillusionment, or illness. It can occur between friends, teachers and pupils, or in any other relationship in which one person tries to make himself as fully pres-

ent as he can during the painful crisis. Through this and similar experiences we share in the redemptive reality of Christ's
life and death.

So too a person experiences the sacred whenever he over-
comes, within himself, obstacles to a fuller life. He touches
sacred experience whenever, after a defeat or a great difficulty, he begins again, once more incarnating himself into
the flow of life. The sacred is inevitably met when an individual faces hard truths and redefines himself by their light.
He thereby frees himself for a fuller life. The sacred is revealed to the person who looks at the faces of misery, sorrow
and even hope, the expressions which sometimes seem to
make up most of the human race. A person who looks at rather
than away from the tragic masks of life does so with the
hope that manifests a steady belief in man even when he
knows how badly man can fail. The sacred is always touched
by the person who lives life at a deep level.

The experience of the sacred is tied in with man's ability
to sense and understand himself and the measure of his
participation in reality. He must possess himself in a genuine
way in order to give himself in a redemptive manner to others.
An important aspect of the experience of the sacred is that it
permits us to understand ourselves as separate and yet made
for relationships with others. There is a deep quality of the
sacred in our sense of individuality which defines more clearly
the problem and the challenge of forging relationships despite
it. This sense of self makes us aware of the fact that we retain
our separate identities even as we establish close relationships with other persons. The individual is not destroyed
through human relationships. He is rather enlarged, and so
this is a religious experience in a real sense. We are one but
we share that oneness with many. This does not dissolve us
but makes us more aware of ourselves, more capable of reflecting upon ourselves, more able to make our own selves
present to God. This psychological separateness, which is a
condition for personal relationships and for any experience of
the sacred, opens man to the mysterious tension of relationships that is part of the life of the Spirit.

A man must possess his individuality because this gives
him the capacity to be alone in the presence of his Maker

Here he can put into refreshed perspective the dimensions of the full truth of life. That is why sacred places are needed to allow man a time to look more deeply into the essential character of his sacred experience with other persons. Man is a sacred place maker, not to escape life, but to memorialize it. He does this in his churches, at battlefields, and in burned-out towns. This, in the long run, is the great sign of man's encounter with the sacred. He makes sacred those places and symbols which say that here, in this place, man has known life in a fashion that is worth remembering, that he has been himself here, has learned to love others, and has found the Spirit at the same time.

8. COUNTERFEITING THE SACRED

In pursuit of the Spirit men are turning toward their human relationships rather than away from them at this time in history. This, as we have discussed in earlier chapters, has taken place because of the rediscovery of man's basic Christian task of learning to love himself. We have come home again in a sense, back to the Gospels which tell us that authentic Christian living is not in eclipsing the self but in discovering the self. Man can approach himself even when he is sinful. The Christian need not banish himself to an Elba-like exile from life because of his shortcomings. Christianity makes it possible for him to confront and accept the hard truths about the growth he has yet to achieve and to forgive himself for falling short of it. As we redeem ourselves through self forgiveness we also affirm ourselves and thereby free our selves for continued growth.

The essential condition for this continuing developmen in the Spirit is the achievement of a genuine and reliable understanding of our true personalities. We do not grow when we do not know ourselves; we only stagger sideways under the burden of false images. The Spirit is available for every man who earnestly seeks to face and deal with himself as he is rather than as he fancies himself to be. That is where we all fit into the picture of the Christian life, all of us who are in fact, sinners, all of us who need redemption, all of us who long to grow but who may stop short of it because we are afraid of the overwhelming shadow of our own sinfulness Recognition of our imperfection in the human condition i actually the first step toward a true love of ourselves. It i also the first movement toward the relative kind of perfection that characterizes those who live by the Gospels. In other words, we live the Christian life in the only way that it is possible for us, and that is imperfectly.

As we move forward, sensing new depths in ourselves as the Spirit transforms us, we become more aware of the sacred dimension of our human experience. The sacred comes clearest to us at those moments of our keenest awareness of our true selves, our relationship to other men, and our relationship to God. This kind of sacred experience requires a person who lives at close quarters with the contradictions and discouragements of life. This sense of the sacred quality of human striving is unavailable to the shallow personality. He has not been close enough to life, to himself, or to other persons to understand the sacred lining of deep human experience. Those who do not deal with themselves as they are simply cannot understand how anyone could experience the sacred in that which seems, in the old phrase, to be only human. For them life is thin and somewhat colorless, always in need of firework-like diversions to give it some significance. The Gospels, in other words, say that you must live as a human being—you must become incarnate—if you are even to touch or be touched by the sacred.

The sacred, then, is revealed and experienced most fully by those who can enter into the area of responsible human intimacy. Intimacy, as has often been said, refers to a broad spectrum of human experience which is not limited to, although it clear includes, the sexual. It refers to that area of life in which we do come close to other persons, not as unknowing strangers bumping elbows in a crowd, but as separate individuals with a clear sense of our own personal identities. The mystery of intimacy, as sacred an area in life as there is, revealed by two people who can meet within the same circle of life's light and let themselves be seen just as they are. It is a mystery that cannot be understood by a person who has never truly shared anything in life, a sacrament of the sacred only to those who have faced each other unarmed except for faith and hope and love. They break through to this area of living and have the courage to be themselves to face what they are really like without distorting or trying to refashion it in an impossible way. Intimacy is the sacred space in which the Christian vocabulary has its greatest power and significance because it is spoken by persons who know the feel of real living.

There is, however, a two-edged phenomenon in current life which we must observe. It is clear that everywhere men ache to experience life in a more significant manner. They hurt, even when they cannot describe it very well, and they have tried a thousand remedies to cure it. It is the ache of loneliness in the heart, the desperate sense of being at the edge of the crowd of life with nobody to talk to. Men try to warm themselves by strange fires when they are this lonely but they frequently only deepen their sense of alienation rather than their capacity for intimacy. One can only be compassionate toward those men, for example, who kindle a pathetic flame of being close to life through watching others make physical love. Middle aged, silent, and sitting separately from one another, as they are described in the New York *Times* account of the observers of live sexual exhibitions in New York City, they are sad men, searching for something which they cannot even rightly name. It is the same for all the lonely people who invest their hopes and their money in cruises which promise a good time and romance, a friend at last for a person who has never had any of these things. Are there lonelier-looking people than those telling their pathetic tales of being disappointed that the marvels of computer dating have never opened the doors of life and love for them?

There are more things than melancholy faces to tell us something of man's search for richer personal experience. These include the wide variety of group experiences which are labeled as "encounter" or "sensitivity" training. It is clear to any observer that the increase in this kind of activity and participation in it by hundreds of thousands of people constitute a clear sign of an effort to overcome the deadness in modern man's experience of himself and others. The encounter movement, emphasizing the sharing of emotional truths, reveals man as he attempts to heal his alienation from himself and his neighbors. Men want to experience life in greater depth, hence the popularity of this movement. Sensitivity training can be understood as a response to the intel-

ectualization, the overrationalization, of man's environment
in a technological era. Technology seems to have bred the
feeling out of man or muted it to such an extent that men
now actively seek to redress the balance within themselves.
It is not, however, just the machines that have done this. The
forces of extrinsic religion, hardly technological, have also
made man edgy about his own insides. They have trained
him to mistrust his emotions, to shut off part of himself so
that he experiences life in partial fashion. This image of man
has proven unsatisfactory because it is not an authentic reflection of man. In any case, man is trying to break out of the
restraints on his personality which have so dampened his
spontaneity and his capacity for life and growth.

Hardly a small city exists that does not have its sample of
encounter and sensitivity training. These are signs of the hunger for meaning; they are not necessarily the adequate response to the hunger. They reveal man's effort to move away
from the surface of his personality and to come to grips with
others in a more totally personal and therefore emotional
way. Longing to feel again, man is trying, as has been noted,
to cure his epidemic loneliness and alienation. The only long-
term answer to this problem, however, is the kind of life the
Gospels tell us about. Sensitivity training and encounter
group experience are fine if they open man to a deepened
appreciation of himself and of other persons. The danger is
that men may mistake the immediacy of the encounter group
experience for the substance of sustained and responsible intimacy. They will settle for the sentiment, the feeling close
to others that seems to have such powerful effects on group
participants. But they may not grow beyond these to more
consistent living in depth with themselves and with others.
These diminished outcomes are not, of course, inevitable.
They are, however, the dangers which are built into intense,
short-duration experiences which take place essentially out of
the ordinary flow of an individual's life. It is no wonder that
the persons who emerge from them are sometimes not as
deeply changed or as positively freed for growth as they would
like to think. The difficulty, in other words, is that in an
age of multiplied groups and sketchily trained leaders, these

potentially rich experiences may fail to be integrated into the over-all growth pattern of life.

This kind of pressured experience may be a step in the right direction but it may also present man with a counterfeit of the sacred, a coin of interpersonal relationship which looks good enough but which does not stand up under the bite of life itself. The world is presently filled with people speaking the Christian vocabulary, using its most sacred terms in a free and easy way which seems to betray a lack of real comprehension of their substantial meaning. It is not only sensitivity groups which do this. The concepts of faith, hope, and love are found in a wide range of activities from advertising to astrology. The Christian who is digging back into the Gospels for the way of life that is expanded by the Spirit must be aware that Gospel terms are frequently used in a superficial manner even by progressive-sounding people.

Faith, hope, and love are profound words, symbols that serve us well in capturing the meaning of our most significant experiences with each other. They are counterfeit in various contemporary markets, passed on to an unsuspecting world that longs for something better and cannot understand its disappointment when it must settle for something so much less than the original meaning of these concepts. A great automobile manufacturer, for example, markets the faith that people would like to find again by saying that its brand of cars offers you "something to believe in." But faith in cars that are designed to wear out in a few years cannot nourish a man through a lifetime. It can only deceive him, cheapening the idea of believing in anything. Using a big word for a small meaning and playing on human longings in such a way as this is an insult to the real meaning of man.

And hope now comes from horoscopes, the astrologers playing sleight of hand with the stars in order to sustain people through the difficulties and decisions of life. But Aquarian hope is cold as starlight as it weaves a spell of wishful thinking around man, inviting him to trust his future to a fate outside of himself. Hope through astrology makes man a passive and insignificant plaything of the gods whose dignity is only diminished by linking him to the blind forces of the Zodiac

Perhaps worst of all in impoverishing the Christian store of sacred words is the assertion that love comes easy these days. How else but by way of marijuana, that sweet smell in the air that generates a feeling of community and makes you a first-class citizen of the Woodstock nation? Marijuana gives you good vibrations, smoothing over all the conflicts and differences that seem to emerge in everyday life, in making love something that is readily available, part of the better living through chemistry that appeals to so many people these days. But to use the word love as if it meant nothing more than warm feelings is to indulge in a fatal sentimentality that only tricks and betrays the innocent. It is hardly any wonder that people can look at these easy varieties of faith, hope, and love and ask, "Is that all there is?"

Traditional values are debased by the shabby use of words to describe them which have only slowly come into our language. As psychologist Sigmund Koch has pointed out, the words for our most important experiences have not gotten into the language easily. Each verbal symbol has a long history, just as each one has been tested by successive generations. Koch says:

The discriminations preserved and transmitted by natural language form the matrix of all the knowledge that we have. Even the technical languages of science have differentiated out of natural language, and their interpretation continues to depend on discriminations within the natural language. From such considerations it follows that if a word has stabilized a salient, delicately bounded, and humanly valuable discrimination with respect to the universe, then a coarsening or degrading of usage will entail a loss of actual knowledge. An individual's conception of the application conditions for a word is a fact of sensibility. Coarsening of language means coarsening of knowledge, and a language community that uses language in a coarsened way is a community of coarsened sensibility. . . . The low level, mechanical way in which the groupers use glitter-concepts like authenticity, love, autonomy, and the rest in the inflated rhetoric that passes for their theory, but which nevertheless controls the selection of their methods and their practice, at once betokens and promotes a serious impoverishment of sensibility ("The Encounter Group Movement" by Sigmund Koch, the University of Texas at Austin, Convocation Address given at Albion College, Albion, Michigan, December 11, 1969, pp. 27 and 28).

The richest connotations of human encounters, then, have only gradually been compressed into these words that we recognize as sacred. When a man uses them, he can do so either as one who has entered deeply into the human experiences which faith, hope, and love signify, or he can speak them so that they sound false to the ear, because he utters them with no real sense of their significance at all. We live in an age in which many of our most sacred word symbols are, as Koch has pointed out, employed by those who have never entered the depths of human experience at all. The result is a confusing kind of superficiality which takes away the majesty and the meaning of man's human vocabulary and does his nature a great disservice at the same time.

One could make a long list of words used lightly or in such a diluted or distorted sense that they convey very ambiguous and ultimately unhelpful messages. So it is for the person who uses words like *openness* and *truth* without much sensitivity to the many dimensions of meaning that are involved in them. Truth and openness currently possess an abrasive face to these people; they have become aggressive words that dig into one's listeners as if salvation always comes through savage confrontation. Among words frequently used in a distorted and shallow way these days are *community*, *trust*, *beautiful*, *sexual*, and *sharing*. Life demands more than that we merely pronounce these words, or any words for that matter. We can only speak these in their profoundly sacred meaning if they flow from the deep level of our own experience.

Love, in other words, does not automatically come to persons, no matter how intense may be the hours they spend together on a weekend. It takes a longer time than that, more trials to test it, and ultimately the test of the years themselves before we can call it love. Trust is not a game in which we allow ourselves to be blindfolded and led around by strangers. It is far more durable, rooted in what we believe in about each other, and flowing from our ability to stick with one another no matter what difficulties arise. Love is a seasoned word; it speaks for seasoned human experience.

The same reflections apply for our new love affair with the idea of the romantic. We have fallen in love once more with the idea of being in love. Nothing symbolizes this more clearly in 1971 than the motion picture *Love Story* with its enticing but deceptive message about the nature of love. The film's star-crossed lovers never resolve any of the difficult relationships which are depicted. Their idyll is ended by the heroine's quiet and beautiful death. Its wisdom about life is summed up in the twice-quoted phrase "Love means never having to say that you are sorry." It all seems so easy, the heady dreams of attractive youth and unending romance pitted against an older generation that just does not understand.

The problem with this portrayal of love, this kind of insistence that problems are solved by changing scenes, this simple-minded aphorism that you can presume understanding when you don't feel like looking at pain: these undermine the foundations of real love which, although more homely, is far more substantial in the long run than that on view in this movie.

"Love means that you never have to say that you are sorry" is a cruel statement, one that takes all the work out of struggling to reach and stay together in life. But you had better say that you are sorry, if you are a human being who wants to stay in love. Saying you're sorry is using the only human mode of communication that we have when we try to make up for the wounds which we inflict on each other, for the disappointments we visit on each other, for our failures to be as much as we should to each other.

The sacred aspect of love, the demands that make us look deeper into life and commit ourselves to the trying struggle to understand and believe that always takes our breath away: this is the face of redemption as we experience it with each other. It is not an easy experience to realize, one that has sharp edges that we would just as soon stay away from. But the real experience of the sacred is permitted only to those who know that life is more than slogans and the easy use of sacred words. The sacred can only be apprehended by those who have assented to incarnation, not for a moment or a week-end, but for a lifetime. The commitment to incarnation, to living in a profound way in the human condition, brings a man to crucifixion, to a recurring death in the heart of the re-lationships made redemptive by the sign of loving on them. That experience of struggle for fullness is what leads men to resurrection, more life for others and for themselves. The Gos-pels tell us that this is possible for man, that it is hard but that it is not a dream. It is this kind of living that stands up no matter what trial or difficulty seems to interfere. Only the romantic counterfeits crumble under life's constant pressure. What is sacred is richly human and durable enough to outlast even death.

9. INCARNATION AS RELATIONSHIP

If the Spirit does reach us in deep relationships with other persons—and that is a very different thing from the maneuvers of forced or pretended intimacy—then the more we understand about human encounters and the conditions under which they flourish, the more surely we will co-operate with the Spirit. When the last myth has died, the reality of learning to live lovingly with other people will still remain as man's greatest challenge. This is, of course, the truth the Gospels have always asked us to make our own; the Spirit leads us deep within ourselves in order to develop our own personalities fully and enable us to share them with other people. Now all these are beautiful thoughts, echoed over and over again during the age of renewal, but the difficulties involved in understanding the genuine responsibilities of this viewpoint are many. And the problems attached to working this truth out in everyday life are not easily solved. We must look to what we have learned about the best aspects of human relationships to understand the foundation on which the Spirit operates to raise us to the full power of our own selfhood.

What does psychology teach us that assists us in deepening our personal relationships so that we make room in them for the transforming effects of the Spirit? Psychology has, in recent years, devoted a good deal of time to the analysis of therapeutic relationships. Researchers have discovered basic and somewhat simple things which have surprised some scientists as much as our own rediscovery that we experience the mystery of living in Christ in everyday life. Healthy things are always fairly simple. The psychologists who have taken a close look at therapeutic relationships have come to recognize that they are not unique or markedly different from any good human relationship. As a group of researchers phrased it in a study of counseling and friendship, "Counseling and psychotherapy provide a heightened experience of the same dimensions present in friendship and have a more significantly constructive impact than the other sources of nourishment in our environment" (Martin, J. C., Carkhuff, R. R., Berenson, G. B., *A Study of Counseling and Friendship*, 1965; quoted in Charles B. Truax and Robert B. Carkhuff, *Toward Effective Counseling and Psychotherapy: Training and Practice* [Chicago: Aldine Press, 1967], p. 120). Something different happens when persons are in vital contact with each other, something that opens them up to an enlarged experience of life and to a fuller measure of human growth.

A common human thread runs through friendship, psychotherapy, and any relationships that can be transformed by the Spirit. It is obvious that neither good friendship, good counseling, nor the deepest of loves has any exclusive franchise on the action of the Spirit; neither can any of these activities proceed independently of the action of the Spirit. The Spirit, after all, comes to any persons who earnestly seek to give the best of themselves to the tasks of life. As we understand the conditions of relationships in which there is evidence that people do grow, we increase our understanding of the way we dispose ourselves for the action of the Spirit in our own relationships. We cannot force the Spirit to come to us; we can prepare ourselves for his coming and dispose ourselves for his touch. That is the genius of the traditional liturgical emphasis on preparation and expectation for the Spirit, on changing ourselves so that we are receptive and able to respond adequately when he comes. In this soaring theme the liturgy matches and builds on a deep truth of life, incorporating man's deepest yearnings into the symbols that express our life in Christ. Mature liturgy, in other words, is calibrated to an intrinsic faith and does not try to work some kind of magic outside of the normal process of personal growth. The liturgy is at its best, it sings in man's heart when it recognizes and capitalizes on the flow of this growth.

What has therapy taught us about life together at close

range? What goes on when persons have successfully entered the sacred grounds of intimacy, for example, and live consciously or not, in touch with the Spirit? We begin by reviewing the general characteristics which research has indicated as part of any healthy human relationship. These are genuinity, empathy, and non-possessive warmth. We will discuss the characteristics of these in the succeeding chapters in an effort to round out our feeling for the almost self-evident but still elusive aspects of vital living. These are the conditions of incarnation, the faces of the discipline of self that is involved in becoming fully a man.

Genuinity is the great quest of the age. We are bored already with the insistence on relating all personal and public experiences and events "as they are." In the name of genuinity, however, men have insisted on the truth, with as little varnish on it as possible, claiming, as they distort the basic meaning of genuinity, that hostile starkness is the key to successful living. The present somewhat relentless quest for the real is something like the search for the Holy Grail, an adventure that has come to justify itself no matter how it is used or what reference it has to the rest of life. One is reminded of the supposed question of the little girl to the knight. "What are you going to do with the Holy Grail when you find it?" The present intense emphasis on a somewhat insensitive honesty emphasizes the rough-edged movement toward it rather than the human uses of genuinity in building a mature life. There is an excitement in the effort to be genuine that makes it self-justifying for many people. It grants them a freedom of expression and a liberation of impulse in dealing with others which they formerly felt were strictly forbidden. They enjoy the loosened constraints, which, like a killing girdle, once gave a civilized shape to their tempers. Now they no longer need to practice the social graces in a superficial manner. One can hardly turn around in any sphere of life without meeting someone who has abandoned the social conventions of courtesy and politeness for the marvelously self-rewarding thrust for genuinity. That, we are told over and over again, is where it is at.

Most of us are familiar with this kind of encounter. We meet a perfect stranger whose lack of ease makes you feel that you must work at being genuine in the first place. He sizes you up, then fires an opening salvo which may go something like this, "I'd like to know where it's really at between you and me before we go any further. I mean, I'd like to know if you are a real person, or what you really feel like, or we just can't get anywhere together." Sometimes you are surprised because you had not planned on getting anywhere with the other individual anyway. This immediate effort to define your relationship in terms of trustworthy personal verities is a bit forced and, in the long run, often quite ineffective. This urgent effort to establish relationship through the mutual confession of faults and the joint admission of feeling is not the way friendship necessarily begins. This romance with genuinity pervades our culture; it is something of a fad with its own vocabulary of approximately real words and its own style of interpersonal maneuvering. Unfortunately, for many who think they are being genuine, this passionate exercise is not really very genuine at all. They forge themselves into a warhead in the name of love. The aggressive quest for the real masks many aspects of themselves which they do not have to look at while they charge forward under the banners of truth.

Genuinity is more gentle than that; it is also better, more long lasting, and more productive of depth in relationship. Being real does not mean, nor has it ever meant, being offensive. Genuinity that increases the life of people in relationship to one another means a freedom together, not a battle; it signifies a lowering of defenses rather than a vigorous assault on them. Genuinity which bubbles up spontaneously from within the individual is a freedom to be rather than a warrant to attack. Genuine persons are disarming but they are not manipulating. Genuinity does not necessarily give you an electric charge from the accumulated tension clinging to it. A genuine person possesses his identity securely enough to allow it to show through in his dealings with other persons. The genuine individual has dealt with the aspects of his own personality, has called them by their right names, and has integrated them into a balanced sense of himself. It is important to realize that the genuinity which flows from a well-achieved identity has a balanced and rounded quality to it. It is not just a bristling, clenched-fisted self-telegraphing punch at the world.

Healthy identity suggests that the person has acknowledged his strong points along with his weak points, that he understands their relationship to one another, and that he works at integrating them into what he now is. In other words, the individual who is in possession of himself has an understanding of his own life history; he knows the ups and downs of the road to the present. He does not have to deny his psychological history or any of his negative feelings. These experiences are, in fact, part of what he is at the present moment. He senses this, even though he need not express it or give visible evidence of it in his behavior. He has come to understand his own passage through life and to fuse it, in proper perspective, with his present sense of himself. As Erikson has noted, "Identity means an integration of all previous identifications and self-images, including the negative" (*Dialogue with Eric Erikson*, Richard I. Evans, Harper & Row Publishers, New York, 1967, p. 36). It is this kind of identity which reveals the depth of an individual. You sense that he has lived and that he has absorbed wisdom from what he has passed through on his way to maturity. All of this is now available to him, transformed by its integration into his adult identity. When he shares himself he shares all that he has been with others. He is real, partly because he is imperfect and partly because he has learned to grow despite the abrasive patches in his life history. In a man like this you sense that there is something substantial there, something of all the things life offers a man: pain, love, joy, all of them come to terms with by the authentic adult. This is very different from the superficial efforts to be real on the part of persons who are actually estranged from their own experience and who seek rather than share identity in their insistence on "real" living.

The authentic man is the man who has grown. His knowledge of what life is all about gives him a quality of reliability that makes it possible to establish a relationship with him. He is available to relationship because he can make the truth of himself present without effort. When we are in contact with an individual like this we experience the meaning of fidelity. A person who is authentic in this seasoned sense does not shift from tide to tide, or surprise us with his inconsistencies. There is a core of truth about him which, as we develop our relationship with him, we find is deep, trustworthy, and dynamic. This center that we find faithful is more than a collection of long dead truths about himself. The man who possesses his own life history is able to be with us through the wholeness and vitality of his fully acknowledged self. We know that we can count on him, not because he tells us this, but because we sense his steadfastness and his commitment to a basic philosophy by which he lives his life. This is where we sense internalized faith, a dynamic, reliable, but not overly rigid set of principles through which he interprets life and makes his decisions. In this genuinity we experience the power of the Spirit at the heart of his faithfulness to the truth about himself and the world around him. Without this human experience, it would be difficult to grasp or understand the meaning of fidelity at all. Fidelity would only be an abstract notion, incommunicable because of that fact, and so not a very effective force in our lives. Authentic people, in other words, teach us the meaning of fidelity because we experience it through them. We understand the word because we have been touched by their personal expression of it. The Spirit reveals the meaning of faithfulness to us through the persons who keep faith with us because they have kept faith with themselves.

Practical questions arise about the quality of genuinity, the foundation on which everything else builds as far as our living in the Spirit goes. Everyone is attracted by the thought of authenticity. It has been one of the great cries of the renewal period in the Catholic Church. We have discussed some things that it is not: superficial maneuvering and hostile self-presentation. A sense of the falseness of these provides us with a good measure of whether we are growing toward authenticity or not. If we find that we are beginning to use the truth about ourselves as a bludgeon to express some long-pent-up drives of our own, then we are on the wrong road toward being genuine. Genuinity implies that our feelings are available to us, that we do not have to deny them, and that we integrate them into a real understanding of ourselves. This takes work, struggle on our part to be honest, but that begins, obviously, with ourselves. The temptation, of course, is to inflict honesty on others. The honesty of the growing person, however, begins at home. If this is the emphasis, then the individual is almost certain to grow in a healthy direction toward the kind of authenticity that shines out of mature individuals. He will be on the road to a deepened faith as well.

This age has witnessed a revolution in our openness toward our emotional lives within Catholicism. The tight old structure that kept them repressed, discounted, or just ignored has collapsed. It is the crumbling of that psychological structure that has weakened other institutional structures. Now we are much freer to discover and listen to our feelings. This is one of the big life-style changes in Catholicism. Now, with the rediscovery of the emotional, people are concerned with whether and when it is appropriate to express their inner feeling to other persons. These questions frequently arise after a person has had sensitivity training or some counseling education. The novelty of sensing one's inner reactions makes people eager to talk about them. People seem in a great hurry to tell what they are feeling these days. This is an impulse about which, in general, we might still exercise some restraint. Genuinity consists in telling the truth to ourselves, in learning to be able to listen to it even when it is disagreeable, and in understanding the implications and effects of our inner experiences on our relationships with others. When we have a clear view of this, we can express ourselves and be ourselves in a reliable and life-giving way. There is an urge, I submit, to get these feelings out in the open as soon as possible, to tell the other person when we are bored, uneasy, or even when we dislike him. This is another part of the relentless quest for authenticity which was discussed earlier.

This is not to say that we should never admit what we are feeling. We are all pretty good at this anyway; there may be times in our relationships with others when this is extremely important for their continued development or for our mature response to the Spirit. In general, however, we should listen and try to catch the truths of other persons more than we should feel the need to express ourselves to them. When we are maturely genuine, we will not have to ask ourselves the question of whether we should say what we are feeling or not.

We will communicate our genuinity to other persons because we will not be able to hide it from them. We will do this in a more integrated and less self-seeking fashion than is common with those people who have newly discovered the thrill of telling other people what they feel.

Perhaps the most essential quality of genuinity is revealed in the man who knows himself, does not deny any aspect of himself, and yet remains in possession of himself in his relationships with others. This is the sense of Christ's presence which comes through even in the heavily mythologized Gospels of old. He is himself and he responds spontaneously and purposefully to life around him. He is a faithful agent of relationship to others, and is a source of life to them because he makes himself fully present to them. Christ is an example of the integrated man and, therefore, the man, who even at this historical distance, is very real to us. Genuinity is at the beginning of our own understanding of the implications of incarnation; it is strange that the real can wear so many masks. This first step in taking on the flesh of our personalities refers us back within ourselves, to the basic business of being true to what we experience so that our genuinity with others flows from the real person that our interior honesty makes of us.

10. INCARNATION AS PRESENCE

Martin Buber, in his celebrated book *I and Thou*, whose title has almost become the motto for the personalistic search of the age, tells us as well as anybody ever has that the growth of the individual takes place primarily through what goes on at a real level between himself and others:

> For the inmost growth of the self is not accomplished, as people like to suppose today, in man's relation to himself, but in the relations between the one and the other, between me, that is, pre-eminently in the mutuality of the making present—in the making present of another self and in the knowledge that one is made present in his own self by the other—together with the mutuality of acceptance, affirmation and confirmation (*I and Thou*, New York: Charles Scribner's Sons, 1958, p. 249).

The Christian life consists in reducing this somewhat poetic vision to reality. Man enters into the mystery of salvation by the door of his ordinary life. He passes through this to find himself in the midst of the lives of others. He can take this seriously or he can shut himself up in the darkened room of his own concern. When the Christian does take others seriously he commits himself to sharing life with them on a mutual basis. The man living by the Gospels does not just do things for others, nor does he just pray for them while remaining at some distance from their troubles and hopes. The Christian lives with the world, bridging the gap between himself and others through active empathy, this unfortunately jargonish word means that he is able to live and move with others in a sensitive and understanding way. A man fleshes out his own Gospel incarnation through being able to hear and grasp the experience of other persons.

The commitment to empathy necessarily involves the Christian in the dying that means he lives truly in Christ. In other words, the mystery of living in Christ is encountered, not in transports of his soul to another world, but on the hard surfaces of meeting and making ourselves present to other persons. This is something like the challenge before a sculptor who gazes at his ton of marble and sees, with his artist's eyes, the human form locked within it. Gradually this figure emerges, but it is not an easy birth, not even from stone. So we emerge from the marble block of our own narcissism as we chip away at it and struggle to shake ourselves free so that we can be present in life as we really are. The individual who understands that life lies on the other side of the bridges we must build between ourselves and other people puts to death the selfishness which makes him sink down inside his own constricted world. We are linked to the saving power of the crucifixion with every step we take toward other persons. It is painful because it means a step away from our self-paneled interior where we are tempted to remain warm and secure. Making ourselves present means breaking through the crust of our narcissistic self-containment and placing ourselves in the uncertain climate of relationship. Being present necessarily means being present to somebody else. Just being present to ourselves does keep us safe from suffering, but it also keeps us from living.

It is, however, relatively easy to look as if we were present to others when we are still sunk very deeply in our own personalities. A man who does not work to empty himself of his own concerns never does reach anybody else. But he can look good making the gestures of seeming concern and speaking the right words. They just do not mean anything; their lack of significance is communicated clearly to others. People who pass through life in this fashion resemble a handsome young movie star and starlet paired together, not by affection, but by some studio manager to attend a motion picture première. They are there, standing next to each other, but they could never be described as being together. They are worlds apart, smiling for the photographers and interviewers, caught up in the impression they are making and quite unaware of each other. The age that emphasizes appearance the way ours does makes this kind of public self-preening an attractive but fatal temptation.

The Christian's first business as he becomes incarnate is to deal effectively with his own self-absorption so that he may be able to respond to the other with his real self. This stripping of the self of the beguiling mythologies that we employ to get through life is a steady process for the Christian who wants to grow. He does not do this by good intentions; he does it by getting into the unattractive business of discovering and putting aside the psychological defenses which enable him to remain inside himself. For example, he must put aside projection, by which we transfer our personality faults into individuals outside of ourselves. Then they have the problems and we can really criticize them while being excused for doing nothing about ourselves. This is a very distorting mechanism, of course, but a very functional one for the person who wants to shut out life and growth. Life's problems are always everybody else's fault, the unpredictable curse of fate, or bad vibrations from another realm. These are all part of pseudo-magic people still use when they do not want to face the pain of moving out of themselves. This task of breaking through our own concerns is fundamental to any kind of Christian growth both for individuals and for the Church as a people. No further growth can take place until the individual takes this first step. It is a frightening thing to do because it means that he will never be the same once he has broken free of his own self-concern.

The individual makes his way out of himself as he pursues his own identity. This is a long process which is normally fairly well concluded by the end of adolescence. At this time a person emerges as a separate individual, a man with an identity of his own which he is able to recognize, accept, and, therefore, to possess in a relatively mature way. There is a self there now, the victory of the many battles of growth. In this achievement of our identity we experience for ourselves the fundamental Gospel insight on growth: the man who is willing to lose himself will find himself.

The miracle of this aspect of incarnation is that the person who learns to die does in fact discover life and is able to enter into the sacred area of intimacy with something genuine to share. This kind of clear and healthy maturing also renders a man open to the action of the Spirit. In other words, there exist no false barriers, and no serious distortions, to prevent him from being in touch with others and, therefore, from being in touch with the Spirit himself. There is a recognizable man there, a reliable and genuine person, who makes himself present first to himself and is then able to make himself part of the experience of others. He communicates what he is to others; his words and the substance of what he is constitute an integrated message. They fit together and others sense and respond to this. When he meets another he is far more than just physically present. He is alive to the other person, responding to the reality of the other with the truth of himself, making himself present to the other without trampling or suffocating the other with the burden of his own concerns. There is a wholeness to this kind of person and an integrity in his style of relationship which reflect the person's dynamic growth in the Spirit.

We are just recognizing what an extraordinary religious act is involved when a person, grown free of the tangle of narcissism, now places his true personality into the living, breathing presence of another without deceiving or overwhelming the other. A finely integrated mixture of incarnation and death goes into the growth of the person who gives himself redemptively for the concerns of others. What, we may ask, are the qualities of this new presence, this sensitive presence to and understanding of the other person? We do not really take on the body of a man in life until we are able to appreciate the experience of other persons. We do this through a disciplined effort, to sense the meaning of others, to accept it, and to manifest our understanding and confirmation of it. That is a fancy way—unfortunately there are so few simple ways to put that which is so intuitively right for man—of saying that we are mature when we are ourselves and can separate ourselves from our own concerns enough to hear and be with others in life. When we understand, when we put into practice what we mean when we talk about empathy, we are cleansed enough of our own needs and preoccupations so that we do get a clear picture of the other and his world. We do not read into it meanings that come from our own world, nor do we distort it to match our anticipations; neither do we insist that it be reordered according to our wishes. We stand before others and make room for them in our own lives.

Empathy signifies a sensitive awareness to the meaning of others. They make a difference to us in our lives, and we demonstrate our grasp of this in a practical manner. Empathy has been described many times. Indeed, most of us recognize it when we experience it, just as we also feel the disagreeable edges of misunderstanding and do not require a definition of it. We experience empathy when we feel understood, when, in other words, what we are and what we express are received fully and accurately by someone else. This is essential for growth, this interplay between people who mean something to each other. People are helped to grow through understanding because this experience tells them, as nothing else can, that they have been heard, that their life and its meaning have registered in the life of another. This does not demand agreement from the other; it does not necessitate disagreement either. The key element is the experience of being received by the other just as we are. This confirms us in a positive way and does not depend on whether the other goes along with us or not. Growth is cut off by those maneuvers that cancel out our experience of being received, the misinterpretations and expectations that lead people to distort what we are trying to express to them. We experience frustration, the non-redemptive agony of blocked communication when we are misunderstood. This is what happens to us when people impose meaning on us from the outside, the quick and destructive interpretation of us that comes when they do not, for whatever reason, try to look sensitively within our lives.

There are many qualities to redemptive empathy. The first, just mentioned, is the heart of the experience itself. We are in touch with people when others take us seriously enough to listen carefully, and to struggle to catch our full meaning as we try to express ourselves to them. There is something going on between ourselves and people when this process is engaged. That something is what we call life. This empathic exchange, under much simpler names, goes on between a man and woman who love each other and who keep on making room in their lives for the feelings and experiences of each other as the years go by. They grow together, not just automatically, but because they do not tire of the effort to understand. This is the same way with friends, but it can be seen in many other contexts as well. A teacher may free his pupil to learn, not because he fills his head with information, but because he understands the world of the student and thereby validates the student's search for knowledge. It takes place between a pastor and a troubled person who just wants to talk about his grief to someone who will look closely at it with him instead of turning him aside with what can be cruel words of encouragement. Any response that shuts another person out is cruel even when the words are quite pious. The experience of entering into another's life is far more religious than all the sweet words of consolation that have been spoken by men whose thoughts have been far away from the people they were supposedly listening to. Empathy does not leave our message hanging there in mid-air. The response of the other completes our struggle to express ourselves, giving it an integrity that comes through the creative richness of down-to-earth understanding.

Empathy gives us added insight into the concepts of faith and hope as well as love. When, for example, I truly make the effort to understand I do more than just strip myself of my own concerns, important though this process of dying is in the redemptive relationships of life. I am a believer in that moment because I respect the fundamental worth and the potential for growth of the other person. I am faithful to the other as I strive to sense the real person who is struggling to become more of himself in relationship to me. I go beyond some intellectual statement that I am concerned about the other and, in the favorite phrase of the day, put myself on the line for him. I am faithful to him as long as I attempt to find, even in the shadowy parts of his personality where I cannot see very clearly, the outline of the person who is trying to bring more of himself into life. I experience the pressure that faith puts on my own reserves; there are, after all, more direct and less exhausting ways in which to relate to other people. It is easier, for example, to seem to be wise than it is to keep believing actively in somebody else. We can give up on others, and, God knows, they sometimes give us sufficient reasons to do this. Only a person who is transformed by the Spirit senses the many layered dimension of faith that is brought more into focus in these moments of understanding than it is in all the cool quiet chapels of Christendom. Faith is alive when the spark of belief leaps between ourselves and others. Faith is not just giving assent to doctrine; it lies far more in assenting to other persons.

In the same manner, we feel a new understanding of hope, both when we seek to understand and when we are understood ourselves. Hope comes down to a human kind of reaching out, the very experience that is at the core of understanding. Truly to understand is a form of reaching out that is far more stressful and a much greater miracle than Moses keeping his arms stretched out in order to gain God's blessings on the battles of the Israelites. There is a tension involved in real hoping that takes us far beyond the kind of assurance which we speak so simply in so many different settings in life: "I hope everything goes okay." "I hope you get better." "I hope this thing clears up." Hope demands that as men we stand firm in relationship to others and stick with them as they make their way through life. It does not mean that we have to interfere with their lives, take over their lives, or be drawn into their problems so that we are unable to lead our own lives. Hope means we are there, not just in intention, but in the psychological reality which is so powerful and life-giving to others. Hope, like faith, exacts a human price; they are both part of the redemptive suffering involved in being alive to each other. Definitions of faith or hope constructed outside of this fundamental experience of trying to understand others are purely theoretical. They are the kinds of faith and hope that belong to extrinsic religion, whipped up out of wishes and vague longings rather than from the inside of life itself. That is why it is so much easier to believe in mythical gods with magic wands that shower hope like mist on an imaginary world—far easier to believe all that than to try to believe in and live at close range with each other.

The effort to understand does not take a long time. One of the most popular misconceptions about understanding is the presumption that it is time-consuming and so we are excused from using it: we turn to quicker if less effective responses. Understanding only takes as long as it takes us to emerge from our own musings and to make ourselves present in a receptive way to other people. Its length is not nearly as important as its intensity, and that is up to us; it is under our control because empathy, that powerful form of presence, comes from our own efforts and not from a magic world beyond us. We don't really lose anything of ourselves when we give understanding to others. Our own capacity for it is enlarged by the Spirit when we commit ourselves to giving it sincerely to others. When we understand we also communicate our values, a sense of where we have been and what we have had to face, and what we believe in: when we make ourselves present to others, we make all of ourselves available; the best thing for growing people is our presence. Just as we are, unrouged and undisguised, we give them life because we are real—imperfect, uneven, but alive—and everything that is a part of our life somehow touches the other in the moments when we are understanding. We cannot be humanly understanding if we do not possess a store of genuine life experience that allows us to appreciate the struggles of another. It is impossible, or very difficult, for a person who lives only by the letter of the law, or by the book, even if it is a good book, to understand another person. Understanding and its concomitant redemptive effects are transmitted by those who are themselves soiled and scarred by life. They have no need of slogans about "where it is at." They have been to the far reaches of life and have looked into the face of love, knowing its disappointments and its joys, and are ever afterwards able to walk more closely with other men.

When people try to grow, whether it is through a time of grief, the anguish of a big decision, or to heal some wound of love, they do not need somebody else with all the answers to tell them how they should live, how they should pray, or what offerings they should make to pacify the spirits that have plagued them. They need other persons around them, the experience that someone is there who apprehends the measure of their own experience and who responds with the profound gift of understanding. Empathy is a quality of understanding presence which means that someone else accompanies us, generating faith and hope as we struggle to understand ourselves.

This kind of presence is a very serious matter, a powerful experience that vivifies life and changes the lives of other persons. It is not the cheap and shoddy trick of trying to "psyche" other people out in order to gain some advantage over them. There is a good deal of one-upmanship in the world, interpersonal psychological warfare in which people try to see into each other as they would into the possible moves on a chessboard. They do not try to communicate concern or understanding; they grapple for power. Some persons, in other words, employ sensitivity to others as a kind of weapon by which they keep others at a distance from themselves. They build a moat across which they fire warning shots to anyone who might come close to their own private person. There are many reasons for people locking themselves this far away from the most important aspects of life. They are lonely and tragic cases and they need our understanding more than our condemnation. Persons who have been hurt in their relationships with others, especially at an early age, may adjust symbolically to life through some variations on the above theme. They never allow others to get close enough to them to redeem them, and they never open themselves up enough to be any kind of authentic presence in the lives of other persons. Behind the neurotic defenses of people who have been hurt like this there are fearful and timid personalities who have grown accustomed to the dark of living inside themselves. They are uncomfortable in the light of day and they do not seem at times to be able to handle the direct expression of concern and affection which other persons try to give them. They seem to resist redemption. They only do this, however, when they are so afraid of the hurt of loving that they instinctively back away from anybody who reaches in their direction.

These people can only be redeemed by others who are willing to go with them a tiny step at a time, not forcing them too quickly into the rushing flow of life, and yet not abandoning them merely because they are difficult to reach. The world is filled with hurt persons who are hard to redeem, with crippled persons who are afraid to walk again, with despairing persons who almost do not want to hope again. Those who give themselves to the incarnate process of empathic understanding know well its constant ascetic demand of emptying themselves in order to reach and open these people to the redeeming Spirit again. Understanding, this special presence with others, is not a passive phenomenon. We do not just stand there while other people spill their problems all over us. Understanding is an active process in which we work hard at trying to piece together the fragments of feelings which others share with us when they tell us about their lives. To make ourselves present in this way requires a concentration and a quality of self-giving that can only obtain when we are co-operating with the Spirit. We do not make ourselves effective co-operators with the Spirit, however, unless we commit ourselves to the discipline that is inherent in this effort to be understanding. It is not a sloppy or an easy kind of thing to do. Neither is it mere sentiment, the response of our own heart to some troubled heart around us. Uncontrolled emotional involvement goes against the meaning of redemptive understanding altogether, crippling others because we tie our legs together with theirs in the mistaken notion that we must live with them to show we understand their affliction.

One of the hardest lessons of understanding is the realization that it is not synonymous with this style of emotional involvement. Few persons, except the most heavily defended, escape the experience of emotional involvement throughout a lifetime. Once burned is twice cautious as far as investing our own emotional energies in the life struggles of other persons. This is an understandable reaction to a well-known human hazard. Emotional involvement is not easily controlled. It is unavoidable in certain situations where a person cannot totally discount himself as he tries to understand. For example, within a family, the making of ourselves present to each other can hardly be kept free of our own overriding concern for each other. In general, however, an essential aspect of the process of becoming incarnate consists in understanding and accepting the fact that we are separate individuals. There is something sacred about this experience of ourselves as separate and yet related to others as well as to our Creator at the same time. It begins, nonetheless, with the possession of our own individual identity. A personality with runny edges is no real personality at all. This sense of our separateness is essential, as a matter of fact, to our being able to understand and help other people at all.

Only when we maintain our own identity and yet at the same time show that we can sensitively enter the world of another are we mature and redemptive persons. When we fail to maintain our own separateness, when we lose ourselves, in other words, in the other's griefs, then we destroy the very element that enables us to be of help in the first place. We short-circuit faith and hope because we do not maintain a healthy sense of our own identity and have instead become identified with the actual pain and struggle of the other person. When we lose ourselves this way we can no longer be of much help to the other and, indeed, probably will need some help ourselves. The overinvolved person destroys his effectiveness because he does not keep his understanding presence distinguishable from the other person's problems. It may be a long and difficult road to wisdom, but the person who wants to understand must learn that he does not have to experience the feelings of another person in order to communicate an understanding of this experience to the other. He can draw on his own previous experience and sensitivity in order to express his understanding but he need not go through the emotionally disruptive situation with the other person.

Essential to this form of presence, to this dimension of incarnation, is a capacity to hear and understand the current feelings of the person with whom we are dealing, as well as the ability, or at least a good effort, to communicate this to him. We have to be there with them—as ourselves, not wholly identified with them—actively making the effort to see into the world of their experience. We go beyond this and, through any of many possible ways, make it clear to the other that we have received their communication, that we have been present enough to understand. This can be done through the words we speak, or just through the reality of our own inner striving to understand, which says something for us even when we cannot. The manner of our conveying understanding is not nearly as important as the fact that we do understand and make an effort to show the other that we do comprehend what he is experiencing. The message which the other receives from us is, in the long run, a fairly simple one. When we strive to put ourselves at the side of the other, we say, in effect, "I am with you." This is the heart of the understanding experience, the source of redemptive strength that helps the other to achieve fullness. This effort to be with others is an essential mark of the Christian's presence in this world. It can only be expressed by those who have entered into the fullness of their own incarnation and who are not afraid to die in order to make themselves present to others. Christians who learn this can respond to an anguished world, not with the judgmental wrath of extrinsic religion, but with the most potent thing that can be offered to others, the understanding presence that heals as it says "I am with you."

11. INCARNATION AS FREEING OTHERS

Men, broken by the pain they have found in its pursuit, have come to wonder whether love exists at all. Americans especially, who more than any other people in the history of the world have tried to unite marriage and romantic love, wonder whether the love they keep searching for can ever come true. Is it a cruel delusion, they ask, as they survey their divorce statistics and the stress of marriages that remain intact, a poetic notion or a temptress of sorts inviting men to have their hearts broken?

The truth is that most of us seek love because we want to be loved as much or more than we want to love others. It is a hard struggle to break out of that bind and to separate ourselves enough from our own concerns to respond to the reality of another person. When it is all added up, it seems a very tricky business to survive as a human being. We fool ourselves so readily, projecting an image of our own expectations on another, loving a phantom rather than a real person, trapped by the fact that we love the idea of falling in love, and only grudgingly acknowledging that the wreckages of our loves are at times shattered silver fragments, mirrors of our own affection for ourselves. One of the unacknowledged miracles of life is the fact that we ever inch out of ourselves and toward other people. It is hard to explain why we start growing, and the scientists are not much help. They observe and measure it but they cannot tell us why man, as he grows toward his fullness, also grows out of himself and toward others. This painful process is hardly one which man would ever embark upon if pleasure were the only driving force that motivated him. Part of man's destiny is clearly communion with others. He cannot, then, claim maturity until he learns the lessons of sharing his life with another human being. These are the lessons of love, that hazardous lifelong journey that takes us out of ourselves and toward others, that breaks the containment of our small world and invites us to become part of the world of other men. For most of us loving is learning to love, growing in the process, and, by its light, seeing a little more every day of what the world is truly like around us. Love makes us real and allows us to be part of the real world. Love is, in fact, the only thing that makes it possible to live, the extraordinary central experience of life through which we finally come to understand that there is no separation between kinds of loves for those who live by the Spirit, and no dividing line between the profane and the sacred. Love lets us see life all as one piece as it incorporates us into the active reality of life in Jesus.

Love is the most significant and transforming experience that we have of the Spirit promised to us by Jesus. All it requires is a little bit of openness, just a hairline fracture in our bony defenses in order to be touched and moved to open ourselves more fully to the Spirit's action. The redemptive cycle of incarnation, death, and resurrection is in its sharpest focus when we are caught up in the experience of love. Love, as every human knows, makes us vulnerable to each other but, in the process, we are also made vulnerable to the Spirit, torn out of our self-containment, and liable to be hurt. And yet we cannot grow in this Spirit unless we are willing to live in this dangerous open place where we give up our protection. Unless we do, we will never know love or ever have a feel for the life of the Spirit. In this condition of vulnerability we experience Jesus' transforming power and know the impulse to grow out of ourselves and toward union with others, the most difficult and mine-filled path in life. The quest for love is inherently redemptive because it makes us grow up at the price of suffering in order to have a fuller experience of life. Through this we enter, blindly and unknowingly at times, into the mystery of Jesus.

He is not waiting for us in Church, although churches are meant to remind us that he is available to us everywhere. Neither does Jesus wait until we are perfect or until we have scrubbed ourselves clean of human concerns. We do not leave this world, in other words, in order to enter into the presence of Jesus, to become engrafted into some effective kind of relationship with him. Jesus is not at the end of the rainbow, not even an ascetic rainbow; he is not a reward for the passive acceptance of a tightly specified code of conduct. The truth behind all the analogies of the Gospels is that Jesus is with us and that we live in him as we try to become more human, and the only manner in which we can do this is through loving. Jesus is indeed the way, and we find ourselves living in Him whenever we take life seriously, because, for each of us, our own life is the way. We cannot, in other words, commit ourselves to authentic living and find ourselves anywhere but in the true holy of holies as we come alive to the saving power of Christ. This is available to us insofar as we try to unravel the mummifying bands of narcissism that hide our deadness and step forth into life with others.

The real meaning of living in Christ is experienced by those who give their best to the insistent demands of becoming themselves through their lives here and now with other persons. This challenge to reach others with our real selves never ends. Our own lives then become the way in which we experience Jesus; the heightened moments of this come with our efforts to love, the moments when we ache and die as we give up what is false about ourselves and achieve the newness of life that is the sealing of the Spirit and our love. Love is a nagging kind of phenomenon; it never leaves you alone, or lets you feast on it and its satisfactions as a miser might enjoy counting his money. That is a form of sinning against the Spirit, to clutch the experience of love to ourselves and thereby to destroy it. That is the kind of turning in on ourselves that makes us into the living dead, shut off really from each other and, therefore, shut off from God as well. Love keeps insisting that we respond to other persons and that we widen the circle of those with whom we are willing to share ourselves. This is the heart of the transforming love that the Gospels tell us about, the love that is big enough to share with many people.

If love does not let us alone, if it keeps insisting that we grow toward a greater concern and response to other persons, it does something for us at the same time. It makes up for what is wrong with us, cleansing us of our imperfections, wiping our slates clean of the failures that loom so large in our lives before love comes along. We humans live in a very imperfect condition, one that is not made up for by all our good intentions, resolutions, or other efforts to transport ourselves through meditation or some form of distraction to another and more attractive world. There is no escape from the imperfections of the human condition. They constitute the circumstances in which we live and move and have our being. It is an earthy world but it is made fertile by the Spirit, and love is the creative force that enables us to meet and overcome the odds that seem piled so high against us. Only persons who are in touch with love's power can make themselves whole. It is not through avoiding faults that this is done or through avoiding the challenges which expose us constantly to the contamination and the wounds of life. Much is indeed forgiven us if we love much. All we really need to do is to make the effort to love and not back away from the suffering that this will entail, and we enter the truly religious and redemptive sphere of life.

The sacred is not trapped by any other human device. Salvation is not won, and it never has been, by the extrinsic propriety that has passed for religion. This strange mixture of magic and manipulation has really only been a stage in man's growth toward an appreciation of the awesome dimensions of intrinsic faith. This internalized faith is achieved by those who strive to love; faith and hope cannot be isolated from the love that is the action of the Spirit within us. It requires a continued effort on the part of all men and yet it gives us something richer and more durable than all the half visions and pagan heritages that have been accepted as religious at other times in life. The kingdom of God is indeed within us, its gates opening to real lovers, those who keep working at love even when they are discouraged or feel too hurt to keep on trying. These people are caught up in the cycle of incarnation, death, and resurrection; they belong to Jesus and know him in the very midst of their lives.

Love is then closely associated with our ability to believe

in other persons and to reach out to them in sustained hope. The high point of Christian love is found in the freeing kind of love in which we prize the other for his own sake. This is a very difficult kind of love to attain, but reaching it even occasionally makes up for the many times we may fall short of it. Nothing demands more of a man than loving another enough not to take anything away from the other. No experience demands that we empty ourselves more of our own selfishness than the kind of love in which we give up making claims on other persons and allow them to be separate as well as different from us. This non-possessive love demands about as much as we will ever have to give in life. It is the kind of perfect love which the Gospels say is the sign of Christian presence in this world and the true expression of the power of Jesus in our lives.

Non-possessive love does not come about spontaneously like Charles Reich's Consciousness III, which seems to bloom without effort. Non-possessive love takes work, constant work, for those who are willing to live life in the depths rather than in the shallows. A sacred truth is revealed to those who try to grow to this kind of love. They enter into the quivering fullness of experience that a person feels when he genuinely and maturely gives himself up for the one he loves. There are limitations to this of course, in the neurotic need to be a martyr, for example, which we find in the lives of some people. That is not what non-possessive Christian love looks like. It is never, in fact, a one-way street, with one person doing all the dying for the sake of the other. Non-possessive love takes two people, each having an equal share in giving and sustaining its life. They live a mystery of dying and rising together in a thousand different ways. They live and grow in Christ and know the sacred at first hand. These people understand why life comes to the man who is ready to die and why it is denied to the man who strives only to protect his life.

Non-possessive love is a very high ideal. It is a strange thing that the institutional Church has approved it so tentatively and cautiously, as though it were a power that could easily slip out of control. Uneasy churchmen are, in a way, wise to understand this because non-possessive love is something that they truly cannot control, and they have no business trying to control it. The task of churchmen is to encourage people's growth toward this kind of relationship with others. They can best do this by creating the conditions in which people can come to learn of the demands of living in Christ. These cannot be written down in a series of laws because mature Christian love cannot be contained in regulations. The experience of the Christian community confirms its members' feeling that religion must offer them something more than regulations, that it must take them deeply within themselves in the context of the experiences which dominate their lives.

For most people, the important struggles of life center on love and its infinitely tangled problems. The Church must support people in learning the lessons of love by revealing to them the fundamental truth that as they strive to love they actually enter into the life of Christ. They should be helped to understand that the community they create out of their willingness to share life with each other is the true presence of the Church in this world. The institutional Church is challenged now to reacquaint itself with the fundamental reality of the sacred and saving experience of people trying to love each other more fully and more selflessly. Its business is to promote that and to make room for the community that will flourish when men have learned to recognize and love each other in a non-possessive way. The Church should be willing to give up everything else in order that this might come to pass.

Non-possessive love demands the best that is in any man, drawing out of him his richest possibilities, shaping him as an authentic instrument of the Spirit. It demands the same from a church that preaches the Gospel of love. It presses it, in other words, to be as true to itself as it can be and to re-fashion its institutional aspects so that they are truly expressive of this value. There is no greater danger, of course, for any one of us than that of affirming this in theory and departing from it in practice. What, then, does non-possessive love ask of the individual and the Church that understands itself as a community of persons?

There can be no love at all except in the lives of persons who take the meaning of incarnation seriously. The life of the Spirit is lived between people rather than in some splendid isolation; the spiritual life is not some other layer added on to our experience. We live in Christ as we grow as men. Any ideas or vestiges of attitudes which distort or dilute these convictions about the heart of life actually obscure our understanding of man and his capacity for deep and abiding love. A church, then, must be ready to set aside the faulted templates that it has pressed down on human experience over the centuries. It must, for example, do more than say that it has made mistakes in dealing with man in the past; it must correct them in the present by its penchant for controlling men and commit itself to freeing men for living. Even an effort to do this sincerely would be redemptive to its effects on the human race.

This leads a person or an institution to re-examine the conditions it builds into the relationships which it established with man. These are the *ifs*, the *ands*, and the *buts* that we can very quietly make the conditions of our response to others. For example, we all know how easy it is to set up conditions for whether we will enter into life with others or not: "I will love you *if* you love me in return," "I love you *but* you had better be the kind of person I want you to be"; the list of these is endless. Now it may be quite natural for us to begin our relationships in this manner. Relationships, like everything else, are meant to grow and to pass through and out of this conditional stage if they are to be mature. This movement away from what psychologists call "the conditions of worth" is the path of non-possessive love. To achieve this love that is given freely to persons no matter what they are like and no matter what they feel toward us is no small accomplishment. Non-possessive love requires a sensitive awareness of our own subtlest feelings, a possession of ourselves, in other words, that is so complete that we know the eddies and currents that move us to react in specified ways to others. Only when we let ourselves feel these things—and they may include a variety of feelings as divergent as anger or erotic fascination—only when we know what is really going on in ourselves can we come to terms with these forces and control them so that they do not control us. These are the emotions that can, in fact, cause us to react to others in a highly conditional fashion, seeking to possess them in one way or another to satisfy ourselves. This is what must die in us if we are truly to free others to find and lead their own lives. A person, or a church, commits the self to a constant dying in order to be a source of life for other people. Only those who know themselves thoroughly can possess themselves enough to lead authentically redemptive lives. They know just what they must yield up about themselves—just what the price of growth is—in order to give themselves away.

The person or the Church that believes in non-possessive love must also believe in letting people have lives of their own. This is as hard a thing as there is in life: the willing realization that our children, our loved ones, or our friends are not our possessions. They are not comfortable fixtures which we can rearrange to suit ourselves within our own life space. They have a right to experience their own separateness and the sense of responsibility for life that comes only when they do experience it. All the sweet talk we may make about love and peace does not amount to very much if we are not really committed to the kind of Christian freedom that is the birthright of every Christian. The tendency to be a fascist is not buried very deeply; one can sense it struggling to get out of some of the most self-conscious liberals. They like to control others, and maybe we are all tempted to do this at times. Whenever we fail to give people freedom, we fail really to love them. We miss the chance to grow and to give growth and step aside from, rather than deeper into, the life of the Spirit.

The idea of loving others without charge, of giving others enough space to make their own way while we still stick with them: these are as revolutionary now as they were when Jesus spoke and lived out these notions. They are the hardest lessons in any life. In many ways, they are the only lessons the Christian ever needs to learn. When he truly makes just a good effort to love this way, he opens himself to the redemptive power of the Spirit and there is nothing that can stop his growth. Neither is there any force, not even death itself, that can overcome his freeing and redeeming presence among other men. It is the Church that gives up everything else—

and how many of the conditions it has placed on its service would it have to abandon!—in order to love without charge that truly preaches the Gospel to all men. That is the Church which changes the face of the earth and against which not even the gates of hell can prevail.

12. THE BREAKING POINT OF THE GOSPELS: LETTING OUR COMMUNITIES DIE

Perhaps nothing in the post-conciliar experience of American Catholicism points to the ultimate challenge of non-possessive love more clearly than the concern that has been expressed about the meaning of community. In pursuing the discussion we find ourselves right up against the challenge that internalized faith puts finally to any group of Christians: are we building a community that is for ourselves, or are we building one that will make room for all men? There are many sides to this question. It is, for example, quite understandable and praiseworthy for Catholics to want to preserve certain aspects of their communitarian achievements, and to be proud of the accomplishments of their distinctive contributions to their various cultures. To write all this off as unimportant is unwise and immature; to think, however, that the transformation of a Catholic community is necessarily tragic may be just as unwise. Catholic communities make no Gospel sense if they live only for themselves, or for their own traditions, no matter how praiseworthy. Catholic communities come to life in order to die for the sake of the life to the larger community around them. This is the breaking point of the Gospel message: are we willing to die that much in order to share what we believe is good news with other men? This challenge is what makes the Gospel life distinctive. It affirms the worth of our traditions and the validity of our previous growth. Then it asks us to sacrifice these, if need be, in order to enlarge the reality of the community of the Church, to make room for strangers and other traditions that dislocate our sense of identity and make us seek a larger sense of ourselves.

During the past year a distinguished Catholic scholar raised a voice of concern about the splintering sense of community among American Catholics. In his epitaph for Christian community (*America*, May 30, 1970), James Hitchcock writes that "the central crisis of the Church is really the breakdown of community, the diminishing sense Catholics now have that they really do share a unique identity and distinctive values." Folk-Catholicism has been laid to rest before its time, before we realized what we were doing in yielding up the symbols and customs we might proudly have celebrated with banners proclaiming "Catholic is beautiful." Professor Hitchcock's verdict: "partly murder and partly suicide."

He is right in saying that something is dead, but I believe he is wrong in raising such a Rachel-like lament. The community that he describes so brilliantly has been broken open largely by forces set in motion by the Spirit. The inevitable destiny of any Christian community is found in yielding itself up for the sake of the larger community around it. Only a community with a definition far too narrow for the Gospels imagines that it must cling jealously to its own particular cultural flowering. Indeed, as Hitchcock mourns the loss of the symbols of our most recent American Catholic cultural experience, he does not seem sensitive to the fact that the Church is undergoing, possibly with greater consciousness than ever before in history, the reality of Christianity's most profound sign and symbol, the experience of death and resurrection that is at the constant counterpoint of the life of the Spirit.

To overidentify the Christian message with any particular cultural development is to misunderstand the dynamism of the Spirit which, if our faith is to be genuine at all, bids us to move out of ourselves for the sake of our brothers in the human family. The Church's redemptive work is not a distant magic; it takes place through the lives of the Christian people whose most difficult challenge is to empty themselves always for the sake of other people. The Gospels open us to a life of going out to men, and this truth defines our lives as pilgrims and missioners. The last thing a Christian can ever do is think that he can build a community just for himself. This is not to say that he should despise his traditions or cultural inheritance. It is to recognize that the Christian must always be ready to step out of these, to put them aside for the sake of men who need him and the good news Jesus taught us. The dynamism of death to self in order to give life to others is the distinctive value that makes Christians recognize and give support to one another in serving the human family. This is the source of communion for Christians that enables them to see beyond their own culture with a generous compassion for all mankind. The Gospel dynamic of death and resurrection makes it imperative that Catholics especially be ready to break camp in order to continue the pilgrimage of service that is essential to the nature of the Church.

The Church is Catholic in the most fundamental sense it never sums itself up under any particular sun; it is constantly struggling, beneath all the deceptive and distracting cultural overgrowth of history, to open itself to all men and all traditions. It may be the only truly transnational community that the world has ever known and, if it can be true to this commitment to all races and styles of life, it can supply the sense of community that is so desperately needed at this time in history. Individual communities, if they harden their shells or burrow underground to pursue only their own interests, are enemies of the Gospel which, if it is to be preached anywhere, should be from mountaintops rather than in hidden places. No matter how rich in tradition, it is right and just for Catholic communities to die to the elements that keep them from making room for other men who need the strength and healing of the Spirit. This notion, the burning notion that makes Jesus' teaching unique, demands that we give away freely what we received freely, that we live openhanded and loving lives in which we are always giving ourselves over to death for the Gospel's sake.

Right now in history, the impulse of the Spirit is to break again the mold in which successful Catholicism finds itself. And nowhere in the world has Catholicism had a more flourishing existence than in America. We Catholics have a proud tradition in North America, but the last thing we can do is cling to it as the singular model of the Church's life. The great crisis of the Church centers on whether it can let certain transitional forms of Catholic community die without making the mistake of thinking that this means the end of

Catholicism or the shattering of our identity as followers of Jesus Christ. It is, in fact, a moment of insight and choice in which we can recognize that our present agonies are essential to anybody living the mystery of Christ and that we must give ourselves over to it if we are to achieve and share the giving of new life that is resurrection. It is a moment, in other words, to deepen our faith rather than feel that it has slipped, like a good thing we didn't want to lose, out of our hands.

The Church experiences the mystery of Christ only in the nerve endings of its members. The people are indeed the Church; what mature Christians feel happening in their own religious lives gives us the clues to the meaning of the action of the Spirit. We would recognize it more readily and feel more united if our present experience were one of persecution. We would be keenly aware of the fact that the pain and suffering in our lives was not random but was linked to the redemption of the world. We would be told this from a thousand pulpits. This kind of experience would be a source of identity and would motivate us to support each other in our struggles. The present Christian experience, however, is different but no less real and no less the action of the Spirit because it is seeded with the confusion and struggle that always go along with growth. We fail, as did early Christians one can only suppose from Paul, who had to keep pointing things out to them, to understand what is happening to us and we fight against it when we are not fighting with each other. We are presently asked to move out beyond what has become comforting and familiar into a newer and deeper expression of our faith as a way of life that makes room for all men. The Christian lives on vision, not on memories. And right now he is asked to be different, at a high price of sacrificing many things he has grown to cherish, in order to make the Church more fully present in the world.

Precisely because it is difficult for us to recognize the redemptive reality of our present experience of what it means to be caught up in the mystery of Christ, we try to save ourselves from the process. We are always looking back on moments of Christian awareness, as though the early Christians had a much keener appreciation of their membership in

Christ. Or we are always looking forward to some great moment in or near the end of time when we will finally be purified of our distractions and know even as we have been known. We end up missing the present, branding the breakup of the Catholic culture as betrayal, soft-thinking, seeing it, in other words, with anything but the eyes of faith that reveal its true meaning as a necessary aspect of the death we undergo in Christ in order that other men may have a share in the life he came to give to them.

This failure to sense the meaning of our painful present also makes it clear that we have had very undeveloped notions of the mission of the Church and the nature of its communities. The contemporary crisis in the Christian community allows us to look more deeply into these themes and to see how they reflect a religion that is also less than fully developed. This is not merely to describe the past; it is also to understand that we are in a period of great potential growth for religious faith and for a concomitant deepening of our understanding of Christian mission and Christian community.

Mission, for example, has been identified in a very narrow way as the generously motivated exile of fine young Catholic men and women whose distant journeys were made in behalf of the rest of the Christian community. Mission was essentially a heroic enterprise, an extra thrust which gained admiration, sympathy, and support from the Catholics who stayed home in their own community. Theoretically and practically Christian mission was carried on somewhere else with remarkably different people while the essential business of the Church took place at home. Indeed, to this very day, one of the techniques for raising funds for the missions lies in stressing how different peoples from other lands are. How convenient to have missionary groups willing to go off to these far places which are so strange when compared to the Catholic culture of, say, the United States. As long as mission means something out there, something heroic but something extra, the Catholic culture that so perceives things has a very limited understanding of itself as the Church. The Church is essentially mission, ordered always to going beyond itself wherever it is found; it lives in and for itself at its own peril. Part of the reason that the Catholic culture which Professor Hitchcock

lls community is disintegrating rests on the impulse to break
rough its insulation and to reach out to serve human need
l around it. This is the missionary impulse of the Spirit
wakening men to an enlarged sense of what the Church is
d moving them to do something about it.

Obviously, lots of things near and dear to those reared in
predominantly Catholic culture will collapse as the de-
ands of this missionary impulse become clearer. It is not an
sy thing to open oneself to the values and traditions of others
one must indeed do if one would make room for all men
one's community. This is, in fact, the breaking point of the
ospel, the test, in a sense, of whether our faith is external
internal, a faith to be shared with all or one to be saved for
urselves.

One of the great puzzles identified by psychologists like
ordon Allport and Milton Rokeach is the fact that many
eople who identify themselves as religious are also deeply
ejudiced and discriminating in their behavior toward other
eople. It is no secret, no matter how we explain it, that some
eople who identify themselves as Catholics are highly prej-
diced and capable of the hate in response to fear that is
enerated by people who are different from them. These peo-
e, according to Allport's helpful insight, have been given a
ith too narrowly circumscribed and too closely identified
ith the interests and advancement of members of their own
hnic and social class. The faith of these people has been left
n the surface by religious formation which has made religious
tivity consist largely in attitudes of acceptance of Church
thority on the way they live their personal lives. It is difficult
r these people to internalize their religious faith and to see
d accept its implications for their attitudes toward people
other races and religions. But this type of problem is famil-
r in the Catholic culture of the United States, the now
assing symbols of which tended to reinforce the "us against
em" isolation of the externally religious members of it.
uspecting Protestants, disliking Jews, and telling blacks to
ull themselves up by their own bootstraps are only a few of
e attitudes which, if they are understandable given the
vel of religious formation experienced by many Catholics,
e nonetheless unchristian and incompatible with a mature

Christian community. These kinds of feelings, reflections of the fact the American Catholic culture has been an unfinished accomplishment at best, are part of what has to die if a broader based and more mission-conscious phase of Catholic community is to come about. This new community will rely less on an identity that comes from sociological realities and more on one that springs from theological realities. A renewed Christian community with a deeper faith and a more inclusive stance and respect toward others will be part of the resurrection experience for the present generation of Catholics.

A further difficulty connected with the communities that flourished within the Catholic culture of America is manifested now in the great concern and frustration connected with developing what is called community among groups of priests, religious, and lay people. Professor Hitchcock seems to regret, for example, that religious groups whose members seemed to get along under the old styles of religious community now have severe difficulties when they are supposed to be motivated by love. Actually, the widespread difficulty of living more normally together that has been experienced by many religious points out the fact that what existed under the old Catholic culture dispensation was not community at all. It was the careful engineering and conditioning of relationships that were hardly human at all. There was little talking, a prohibition on close friends, and a rewarded docility toward authority that, taken in combination, reduced conflict to a minimum. But that is out of *Walden Two*, not out of the Gospels, and the Catholic experience of controlled communities could tell B. F. Skinner something about the inevitable collapse of these under the healthy human wish for something more profound than efficiency and good order. The demise of convent living, the restyling of much of religious life: these are advances, not without their living problems, over the former communities that stifled so much life.

One of the peculiar characteristics of many of these religious and clerical communities was their talent for defining themselves and their members not only over against the rest of the world but over against the rest of the Catholic community as well. Nothing has been more antithetical to the

Gospel vision of community than this sanctified tendency to look on priests and religious as apart or above the rest of man. The Catholic community had problems of its own in perceiving salvation as their own special reward, but this was intensified to an amazing degree in the subcommunities of priests and religious. Theirs was a life of perfection with a clear if subtle focus on their own salvation. Catholics in general and the Church's servants in particular constituted a community of the elect. The harder sayings, the more demanding regulations, the sacrifices in marriage and celibacy: all these were well worth while in view of the rewards for these in the life that would come afterwards. It is interesting to note that Dr. Gordon Allport, the late Harvard psychologist, cited the notion of the elect as one of the sources of prejudice within Christianity. It is quite possible that the Catholic culture self-image as the chosen community made it more difficult for its members to be open to other people on an emotional level. Perhaps this feeling was unavoidably associated with many of the symbols of presumed unity such as fish on Friday and the Mass in Latin, which we have given up. If we have lost some of the sense of unity which these generated, perhaps we have also lost some of the self-assured feeling of election which made us so focus on our own salvation and on the world beyond this one. In other words, many of these symbols may have had exclusionist connotations since they served to define us as a specially chosen group of Christians who would have special protection if we fought the good fight in a bad world.

The exclusionist mentality ran deeply in the subcommunities of the clergy and religious. Perhaps the most famous example of this bias is the clerical mind. One has to step back and shake one's head a little at the special niche that was carved out for the clergy over the centuries. This special place within the Catholic community has made the clergy a highly visible target for criticism as much as anything else. It also led to making unrealistic demands on them. The great distortion, however, lay in their being made so separate from their people. Much of the present uneasiness in the clergy is not really disaffection and disloyalty as much as an effort, with a hundred different faces, to bridge the gap that has developed between priests and people, a gap that no reading of the Gospels can possibly justify.

This is not to say that the priest has no identity of his own or to suggest that it should be fused totally with that of the Christian community. Some of these vague notions about the priesthood are merely a reaction to the excesses of the long-standing relationship gap between priests and the community. The priest finds his identity, if he is ever to find it, in the midst of the Christian community, in relationship to the people he is called to serve. The organizational aspect of the Church, however, in uncounted ways, from tracts on spirituality to the special sections of canon law has defined the priest and bishop over against the rest of the Christian community. They were even to be buried with their feet facing a different direction from those of the laity. This has led to disillusionment when they have failed to be as special as they have been made to seem. They also suffer heavy criticism when they fail to produce the kind of leadership which this carefully prescribed distance from their people often made it impossible for them to exercise anyway. Most exclusionist of all results has been the development of the clerical attitude in which priests and religious begin regarding themselves as special because the people regard them this way. This has broken down considerably, but it is difficult to imagine that it was ever a good thing, or even a Christian thing, to have priests and religious believe that they had special keys to the kingdom, a separate and more highly differentiated spiritual life, or that there would be a variety of distinctions awaiting them even in heaven as a reward for their special state in life.

The clerical specter looms up even now at times in many priests' senates and associations which have had such an uncommonly difficult struggle in trying to break the vicious circle of self-concern which has so dominated their liberations over the last four years. Once the issues of clerical retirement, working conditions, and better pay are treated, each senate or association seems to undergo a crisis. This crisis springs from the soil of the narrow world into which the clergy have been forced so that the aspects of life which are their chief concern are tied closely to their own form of life. There is little response to the broader vision proposed by some of their leaders and a reluctance to relate in any equal kind of way with the laity. In fact the laity in the older Catholic culture prided itself on a complimentary mentality, in which they paid the bills, fixed the parking tickets, and smiled on seminarians and newly ordained as the finest flowering of their Catholic communities. No one can blame either group for this interlocking set of attitudes. That clericalism, with all its exclusionist overtones, is antithetical to Christianity and that it is crumbling under the dynamism of the Spirit that is reforming the Church are the realities beneath some of the observations made by Professor Hitchcock. The passing of the Catholic community which felt itself to be the elect and the even more elect clergy and religious communities within it: this is hardly to be mourned too much. Much of the concern about celibacy is connected with the fact that this charism had been so diminished because it was regarded as an elect state rather than a mode of service to the community during the history of the Church. Indeed celibacy is championed, in a strange contemporary example of the exclusionist mind, as the great distinguishing mark that makes the religious vocation distinctive. The echoes of the exclusionist attitude are found in those religious who, in trying to define their community life, ask over and over again, "What makes us different from other Catholics?" The gradual death of the clerical-religious mind will be necessary for the further growth of the Church.

The Gospels invite us into a way of life with our fellow man and they ask us to yield up those things which make us selfish, the things that make us want to build or hold on to a community that is just for ourselves. They dynamic of redemption is at work in us as we try to move out from the shadow of a confining Christian community and into a whole new set of relationships, far more openhanded and generous, with the world around us. If we take this step in the growth of the Church seriously, we must confront ourselves and the depth of our faith as we have seldom done before. This is exactly what is at stake at the present moment in the history of renewal. The Christian community which could co-exist with anti-Semitism, race prejudice, and other undeveloped moral outlooks, the community that saw itself as chosen and its servants as the most chosen of all, is opening up. In the process we are all asked to open ourselves up to understand the implications of the mission we have to the human family through baptism in the Church.

The great Swiss psychologist, Jean Piaget, through his careful observations of children, tells us a good deal about the struggle an individual goes through to develop a sense of his membership in the world around him. It is a long and slow process for a man to come to an authentic understanding of what Piaget terms *reciprocity*. This is our ability to perceive others as individual persons existing distinct from us with separate rights and traditions whose values may be equal to those which we hold dear ourselves. It takes years for a child, for example, to begin to be able to look at other people in this way. When he is six or seven and you ask him to draw two circles to represent Switzerland and Geneva, the child will draw two circles side by side. A concept of belonging to co-extensive communities is as yet beyond him. He can speak of himself, the places he has been, and the people he knows only in very self-referent terms, that is to say, in terms of whether these people or places have been sources of pleasure or satisfaction for him. It takes a long period of growth and education before he can understand that citizenship in a city and a country at the same time do not contradict themselves.

A man must gradually de-center himself to achieve maturity. The big challenge for men, as many psychologists have noted in commenting on Piaget's work, is to pass through that point where they sense the demands of a relationship that takes them beyond the borders of their own country and their own heritage. This is the kind of loyalty on a supranational basis for which, as Allport once noted, the world has no good symbols. The appropriate symbol for this, the community to which we all belong, should be that of the new Church. This is the community which understands its presence as co-extensive with the world and knows that there are no longer any distinctions to be made, either Greek or Jew, either slaves or free men, when Christians live by faith. This is not a dreamy, Henry Wallace-like attitude. It is a challenge which Christianity has always posed, the challenge to de-center ourselves, to break camp rather than cluster around our own campfires, and to try to build the community of the world which is so desperately needed at the present time.

Much is made in our day and age of our duty to be faithful to the Church. Not enough is made, I suggest, of the Church's being faithful to its people. The death of the Christian community, that community which set us off, made us separate, gave birth to the dizzying dreams of being the elect, and generated the clerical and religious mentalities is dead. This is one aspect of the death-resurrection mystery in which we are caught up together at the present time. The Church is not faithful to its people unless it allows this de-centering process of growth to continue; it is not faithful to the Gospels if it fights to preserve what should be yielded up for the sake of all men. The Church in mission is called to give community to all men rather than hold on to it for itself. All narrower understandings of Catholic community must be yielded up in view of the plight of men who are lonely and alienated everywhere, men who have never been so hungry and thirsty for the nourishment that only the Gospels can give. The old Catholic community has indeed died but only to energize us to understand the enormity of the challenge to our faith and commitment to the world that we will experience over this next generation. If the world is to be a community, if it is even to celebrate the dawn of the year 2000, it may depend on our willingness always to die to the Christian communities which, at best, have been only sketches for the Church we are called now actively to build.

13. PROBLEMS FOR A GROWING CHRISTIAN: TEMPTATION AND SIN

Temptation and sin have been reliable staples of preachers throughout history. These topics have been high on the list of concerns for those who have emphasized extrinsic faith; these subjects have always been related more to fear and hellfire than to growth and wholeness. But temptation and sin are related to growth, the one a test of it just as the other is a rejection of it. Temptation and sin are not isolated, win-or-lose experiences which come at us out of some dark and devilish pit tended by Satan. Temptation and sin, in other words, are not alien and extrinsic forces thrown across our path by the Bible's numbered beast. For most of us our experience of sin and temptation is closely related to our own personalities, as close to us as our own possibilities. They come to life on an inner stage where, by the light of our own awareness, we decide for ourselves just how alive and loving we are going to be.

Sin can be talked of in an objective way; no one would seriously argue with that notion. Sin, however, must be thought of, as we have come more fully to understand in this century, as a subjective thing, a personal thing that bears our own seal. That is what the old effort to specify the conditions for serious sin really tried to tell us. The question of adequate reflection and full consent of the will meant that whether we sinned or not was up to us. We could only sin freely just as we could only save ourselves freely. Temptation and sin show how we use our freedom. They are signs of the style of our lives, of its thrust and meaning. Our temptations are like a fever chart registering the values we live by and the integrity of our commitment to our own growth and the growth of those around us. Temptation and sin, in other words, are dynamic and significant aspects of our human experience, the moments when we can sum ourselves up and make the choices that define our lives.

If ever a notion has become old-fashioned, however, it is that of temptation. It still hangs like a darkening daguerreotype in the Christian gallery, where people like to look at it as evidence of a historically interesting process rather than as a representation of anything real. Modern, free-flowing moral forms, in which self-discipline seems an enemy, catch all the attention these days. The current cultural codes does not allow but command a response to any and every impulse. The notions of delay of gratification or the control of one's inner stirrings are judged to be puritanical residue at best. Some demythologizers of the Gospel would have us believe this as well.

This supposedly free-and-easy approach to drawing water from all of life's wells may, as many observers contend, be a kind of overreaction in the present to the overcontrol of the past. Few things used overkill in this regard as powerfully as the forces of the extrinsic religion. Now there is a lot of talk about how a man must do everything and taste every possible experience if he is really to be alive. Indeed, as a concept, temptation is associated more with the perils of affluence than the building of character. It is invoked on the presence of the rich foods and the richer dessert carts that threaten the contemporary slim books; it is manipulated skillfully so that men end up buying what they cannot afford to give the impression that they can afford it. There are many reassuring slogans about living a little, spoiling oneself justifiably, and about how long we will be dead that make it easy for us to deal with temptation according to the formula of Oscar Wilde by yielding to it.

Temptation is not dead, however, even though the word may not be much in vogue any more. Temptation is a real experience, no matter what name we choose to give it, one that we can feel throughout our personalities. It still gives rise to tension, restlessness, and conflict. It is by no means limited to the area of sexuality, although it is real enough there. The struggles of temptation are also felt by men who crave, among other things, power, money, and influence. Our whole picture of temptation posed man, full of yearning, before some forbidden fruit. He either gave in or backed off; he conquered or was conquered. Although this is still argued enough as far as it goes, it leaves out a great deal that is important for a new look at an old problem.

Temptation, in a sense, is not all bad. It is, after all, a sign of life. It should be viewed as part of man's struggle for growth, an aspect of life experience that is essential for his full development. Every man must test his own identity against reality itself. An individual does not grow merely by thinking about it, or wishing for it; somewhere along the line he must measure his self-understanding and his strengths in the contest of life. None of their idle steps to maturity, such as the acquisition of impulse control, can be taken unless a man subjects himself to the tension of making a choice, which is the most important sign of a free and growing person.

To eliminate temptation is to close off one of the avenues that lead men to fullness of personal development. The worst result of these modern day thinkers who would have man do whatever he feels like whenever he feels like it is that this robs man of choice. It despoils him of what is most human about him, his freedom to choose for himself the values by which he will live, and every man born to be responsibly free will have many temptations, even when he doesn't want them and even prays to be delivered from them. The tautness that a man feels inside himself at the high tide of temptation arises because the real issue is always the nature of the choice that he makes. In fact, temptation does not always run at flood tide through our lives. However, a steady flow of choices, some big and many small, is presented to us every day. It is not just in the heightened moments of temptation but in all these decisions that man can choose himself. He can choose something that will add to his growth, or he can choose something else that may detract from or delay his growth. A man does not choose himself once and for all; it is an act he must repeat every day in many different circumstances, and the temptation to choose something less than his full self is always present.

Perhaps that is the underlying meaning of every temptation, no matter what the specific setting. We can choose what makes us bigger or what makes us somewhat less, whether it is the question of failing to tell the truth, or of cheating at our job, or even of cheating on our spouse. The primary temptation asks whether we love ourselves enough to do right by ourselves, whether we tap our full potential or sell ourselves short, whether we possess ourselves fully or let ourselves go. The way we respond to ourselves in the moments that test our strength tells us, better than anything else, whether we have any sense of responsibility to others. We end up either giving more of ourselves, and this means growth, or giving them less of ourselves, and this comes close to the real meaning of sin.

The temptations of Christ in the Gospel are illustrative. In essence, they are invitations to put aside his vocations, to relinquish his sense of mission and all its possibilities, and to settle for power rather than service. Man is always fundamentally tempted to give up what he can really be, to withhold himself from life and thus to deny himself and others the effects of his full self-affirmation. We can hold back in subtle ways, in friendship, for example, or in love, where the demands of faithfulness are put into sharp focus by temptation. The temptation is always for a short-term gain and the forsaking of a longer-range commitment, for something of the instant that impels something more lasting. Moments of temptation ask us whether we are ready to grasp and deal with the deeper values connected with the self and the meaning of life. These are never easy moments, and we can deftly defend ourselves against facing the truth about the many issues involved. We can, in other words, live at the surface of life, never getting into or sharing ourselves with anyone. That is the destructive core of temptation, the slow shriveling of the self that has never entered into life at all.

Wholeness comes to a man not just from resisting temptation, although this has traditionally made him feel good. An individual grows when he faces the full dimensions of temptation and chooses the course that demands more of himself. That is what helps him solve his own true depths and release his true creative powers. We are fulfilled, not, as some contemporaries suggest, by giving into temptation in the name of fuller human experience; nor are we fulfilled, as some ancient spiritual writers seem to suggest, by backing away from life and its dangers, frozen in some pious attitude of resistance; we are fulfilled as we find ourselves through making positive choices that demand more of ourselves. Temptation is an opportunity to make a commitment to one's best self, to one's possibilities to the fullness of life that is promised to all Christians.

Our reaction to any temptation offers a moment when something essential about the Christian dynamic of life is represented. We die of something in view of a richer and fuller life that follows from self-affirmation. These are our redemptive moments that recapitulate the whole of Christian life and ask us to choose it even though it causes suffering, because it inevitably leads to resurrection. The Christian is a free man, and each temptation gives him the chance to proclaim this truth over again. The choice is always very personal and it always has to do with whether we will grow or not.

For example, a closer look at pride, once well known for riding point on the capital sins, shows how the choices involved are rooted in our own personality in the direction we choose to go in life. Pride has, as a matter of fact, fallen, along with the concept of temptation, into disfavor. The probable reason for this is that it was just overused as an explanation for our perversity. When I was in the seminary it was the all-purpose vice, the sure diagnosis for every spiritual illness. Like the common cold, there was a lot of it going around in the old days of ten-day retreats and silent prayer.

In fact, pride was the most pursued of vices, just as humility was the most pursued of virtues. There was at times a kind of competition among the devout to dig out pride from the nooks and crannies of the soul where it readily took root, and humility, to think of oneself as nothing, was the DDT to kill it off. Now, just as we are wary of the overuse of DDT, many Christians are afraid they overdid humility in the battle against pride. The self was always under siege and was valued so little that many discovered that they had seriously undermined their own self-confidence. Small wonder that there is so much talk about fulfillment and the development of the individual personality these days; it is a reaction to the highly negative attacks launched against the self to overcome pride.

Pride still lives, of course, although it is not an intellectual vice, even though it has often been described that way. For that matter, it isn't even all bad. Pride is more a feeling about ourselves than a way of thinking about ourselves. As such, it is the product of the way we use our personalities and the labor and love of life. When we use ourselves well, we have a good feeling about it, a kind of pride that flows from fitting together in relationship to ourselves and to others. That is a healthy feeling, the feedback that is akin to the pride of workmanship, the emotional evidence of a person who is loving himself rightly. A man who is trying his best will experience a wholesome pride that is quiet and filled with peace. That is a sign that a man is living by the Spirit.

Pride that is distorted and destructive arises from false premises about the self. It is a feeling about ourselves that is so inflated and pervasive that it edges everybody else out of our lives. The victim of this type of pride does not know himself, and cannot love himself in an integrated way; he can only defend himself against his own distortions as he wallows in his narcissism. It is very difficult for this kind of proud man to love. He would rather go down in the loneliness of his self-infatuation than make room for his real self or for others in his life. Men have been known to be too proud to fight and too proud to beg; the most melancholy man of all is the one who is too proud to love.

Pride, in this extreme form, chokes off life because it closes a man off from others. The sinfully proud man plunders the personalities around him, feeding himself but failing to notice others. His pride is a defense against seeing the truth of what he does to himself and to others. This kind of pride runs deeper than the vanity that makes a man concerned about the way he looks on the outside. That kind of vanity is common and forgivable; the pride that shuts out others is not so common and is always deadly. It is the great sin against growth.

Indeed, the problem is not the deadly proud man who nuzzles comfortably into the lining of his own ego. It is, rather, that we have so few people with the healthy sense of pride in themselves and that we have so many whose feelings are characterized, not by overconfidence, but by underconfidence in themselves. It is not that they are overgrown; it is that they have not tried to grow much at all. This lack of confidence in people may be partially the fruit of all those years of beating the supposed badness of pride out of them. It may be complicated by the pervading sense that so many things in life seem to have gotten beyond our control. In any case, this lack of trust in the self, this non-pride of self-alienation, is practically an epidemic in Christendom today.

This underconfident person never gets to know himself very well either and so he never really tests his strength in the struggle of life. There is some evidence to suggest that those who never really tapped their own resources hold back from life out of fear of failure. To avoid the painful consequences of a public setback, they do not involve themselves at all. They shift uneasily on the edge of life, waiting for the right moment when no one will laugh at them and no one will criticize them. They use a perfectionistic defense, always putting off doing this or that until they are sure they have it planned so that they will be immune from criticism, but they never get it perfect enough and so they never get very much done either. Waiting for the moment of no risk at all, these people are always on the sidelines but never really in the game.

The really capital sin, if such a term can be used, is this passive and fearful non-participation more than it is any overbearing kind of pride. The mock humility of some of these people covers up their desire to neutralize the conditions of life so that they are never in danger. But that is to turn away from life altogether. St. Thomas once asked the question of whether it would be better to ask a proud or a fearful person to do something. He said that he would choose a proud man, because then at least something would be done. The fearful man, on the other hand, is overcome by caution and he avoids mistakes by avoiding action altogether.

Fear that has not been faced lodges beneath the problems of the persons who have not learned to trust themselves or take a healthy pride in making their best effort, even if it is imperfect. These people have a lot of trouble loving others, too. That is because love subjects us to the biggest risks of all, the danger of being bruised by the ones we love. Right now the world and the Church need people who are ready to run some risks, even the risk of being a little proud, for the sake of loving more. The first step in incarnation requires the choice to grow; one sin against the Spirit is surely this rejection of growth, this unwillingness to enter into the mystery of Jesus which is announced to us in the Gospels. Fear rather than pride, a fear of our own possibilities, makes us give in to the temptations of not really living at all. It is not Satan outside of us who prevents us from entering into and sharing the Gospel life with others. It is rather the fainthearted-edness of those who comfort themselves with thoughts that they are humble when they are really only scared.

14. WHAT IT'S LIKE TO GROW: FIGHTING AND FORGIVING

Many aspects of our lives resonate to the challenge of the Gospel; we can feel it deep inside ourselves when the Spirit challenges us to become more than we are, to grow, in other words, to our full humanity in Christ Jesus. The essence of the life of the Spirit is the constructive growth through which we become more fully ourselves and thereby redeem our existence. An intrinsic religious faith makes us more aware of the constant demands on our inner transformation that are made on us by the Gospel. Perhaps that is why St. Paul described his own experience in terms of being pressed and urged on by the love of Christ. He felt the tension of growth through response to the Spirit, the same experience which we ourselves can sense throughout our being. We know that the Gospel asks more of us than staying out of trouble, assenting to certain formulations of doctrine, or just minding our own business. We are constantly invited to grow and to transform ourselves and the world around us through the power of Christ.

In other words, growth is not just a heroic notion. We know that we have to change ourselves, that we have to deal with our own selfishness and our own temptations to stay on the safe edges of things. We search out our own gifts, deepening our awareness of the need to bring them forth for the sake of the community around us. In no experience do we realize how much we have to change if we have to live by the Gospel than in the challenge to build a community that truly makes room for all men. We come face to face with our shortcomings, our prejudices, and our longings to cling to the familiar, the something that sets us off as separate from others. The Christian impulse does press us to break through the shield we are tempted to build around ourselves and to grow in a positive and creative manner through enlarging the lives of others. Something inside of us has to change if we are serious about living this kind of faith. Sunday Mass and regular contributions have never been really enough to discharge our obligations as Christians. The more we look into this, the more frightening it may become, because the brand of incarnation-death-resurrection is burned into all of these experiences. The Christian is active, alive to the world, and knows that he gives life in proportion to his willingness to put to death his own selfishness.

We will discuss two areas in which we can feel keenly the pressure of the Spirit to transform ourselves and to become something greater and more loving than we are. Many other areas could be investigated. They would all yield, in one way or another, similar evidence of the fact that the Gospels are a way of life rather than just a string of beliefs and that they demand the internal change of heart that opens us to true growth in the Spirit. This is clearly felt in the challenge to fight the good fight of life, a phrase that is hardly outmoded, and to learn to forgive from the very heart of ourselves.

"Do not go gentle into that good night." So wrote Dylan Thomas, the Welsh poet. Rage, he said, rage against the dying of the light. The trouble is that we live in an age in which people have increasingly justified going quite gently and quite passively into more than a good night of death. We have gone a long way in rationalizing our way out of ever having to face and work through pain, anxiety, or even an occasional sleepless night. Better by far to take the appropriate pill that puts pain and bad moods behind us, the prescription that lets us lie down in limbo for a while. No raging here; just a search for quiet and for at least a few moments when life doesn't hurt quite so much. In the same way man can make himself so passive to the Spirit that he hardly seems alive at all; he fixes himself in an attitude of listening because sometimes this is easier than having to deal constructively with the internal obstacles to his own fuller growth. To be meek and humble of heart does not mean to surrender rather than to fight it out with ourselves and the challenges of life.

It seems so difficult to blame modern man, harried and criticized on every side for taking whatever relief he can find. But the Christian might wonder whether he is not tranquilizing himself out of essential experiences of growth when he backs away from the battle with pain that is so much a part of the experience of living in Christ. The Christian learns that he has to meet pain and loneliness head on sometimes. This is not an invitation to masochism or a condemnation of sleeping pills, but perhaps pain can only be conquered by taking it on as an enemy who must be faced down, with quarter neither given nor requested. Man has more resources than he usually thinks; he may never discover them, and therefore never discover himself fully, if he does not enter that pain and suffering that test his depths and test them true. There is a place in life for the experience of pain, not for its own sake, but because it burns the dross off a man in a way that nothing else can.

If a man never fights the battle of suffering out in the open, with full consciousness of what it is all about, he may miss something that is essential to being full grown. He will miss the full measure of friendship which takes on this meaning, not in the past cups of celebration, but in the moments when anguish is shared; he will never know real love because in trying to perpetuate romance he will not face the fierce and lonely moments when lovers can look like strangers to each other; he will not know the full face of life because he has been afraid to look steadily into the eyes of death.

Man estranged from pain will hardly be the figure we have known all through history. He will be like a child overmedicated against the infant diseases so that he never builds up a strong inner immunity against them; the man who never learns to live with pain only makes himself more vulnerable to it. I am not defending the large measure of unnecessary pain that is found everywhere in life. No one in his right mind would do anything but attempt to lessen this in all its forms. I refer to the inevitable sufferings of life, the pains that shape our existence, the pains that must be faced because they cannot be fended off. Man who names the birds and the beasts must put the right name on his agonies if he is to do battle with them and down them.

"We are healed of a suffering," Marcel Proust wrote, "only by experiencing it to the full." Redemption lies, then, in the sifting of our real from the fancy problems and then dealing with both of them realistically. Some people cover their real problems with imaginary problems to such an extent that they never can tell the symptom from the real suffering. They have terrible headaches in place of working through the difficulties of a tangled personal relationship; in fact the headaches excuse them from even understanding where the real problem lies. That kind of person misses the self-identity that emerges when we truthfully confront the real challenges of living. He cannot experience his suffering to the full because he will not let himself see what it is, and so he cannot find or offer redemption through the experience. People are ordinarily afraid that they will miss the meaning of life if they miss one of its possible pleasures; they run a far greater risk of missing its meaning when they shy away from its sufferings.

The Christian is familiar with all of this. He knows that Christ dreaded but actively accepted the pain that was inseparable from his role as the redeeming servant of mankind. Christ knew what men would do to him and neither looked away from the suffering itself nor from understanding the complex motives of his persecutors. He faced and conquered suffering and death; he did not surrender to them. Our involvement in the continuing mystery of redemption bids us to deal with our own personal pains in a similar fashion. This is not the stoic refusal to admit that pain can lay a hand on you. It is rather the Christian's active entrance into his sufferings, his standing up against them or grappling toe to toe with them while the light lasts; that is the way of life because that is the way of resurrection.

The Spirit comes to the Christian who remembers the worth of fighting a good fight and who is not wasting his blows on the empty air. St. Paul spoke of keeping faith that way. Perhaps he meant that his refusal to go gently into the night of suffering was a way of keeping faith with himself and his true identity as a man and as an apostle. The Christian feels alive in Christ when he rages against the real suffering in his life. He knows that it may well be the price of his soul.

One of the fights the Christian will have with himself is the battle of learning how to forgive. Life can seem to him filled with enough hard things, misplays, and misunderstandings of all kinds. Somehow it just does not seem fair that, on top of all these, the Christian is expected to forgive others for their faults. The problem, and the reason that it is such a challenge to growth, is that it is not just forgiveness in words; Gospel forgiveness must be real or it signifies nothing. Forgiveness, according to the Gospels, must come from the heart, and that, of course, is just what makes it so hard. When we do something from our heart we are doing something with our whole person. It is the moment, if the moment is ever to be, when we make ourselves fully present to others. Many strands of Christian experience in the Spirit are bound tightly to the moment of forgiveness. It is indeed the moment of truth in which the depth of our faith is revealed.

Forgiveness cannot co-exist with closing off some inner chambers of personality in which we can keep the fires of bitterness banked until some opportunity for revenge comes our way. Human beings like to do just that, holding on to old hurts long after everybody else but them has forgotten and warming themselves with the knowledge that they have kept some things on file for that great getting-even day. For some of us that makes all the suffering worth while. We can wait, like the Count of Monte Cristo, until that moment of freedom when, blinking into the sunlight, we can take out after our enemies.

The hard part of what the Gospels say about forgiveness is that we must forgive even when we are right. Forgiveness would not make much sense any other way, of course. It is not something for those who never hurt us but for those who do. It is hard enough at times to love our friends, but the thought of forgiving our enemies is downright startling. That is what makes Christianity so different from any of the other religions that the world has ever known. It does not ask us just to put up with and accept life's betrayals through some kind of sweet and quiet contemplation; it challenges us to be active, to go out and meet our enemy, not to spite him, but to embrace him. It is in the question of forgiveness that we experience down deep just how much genuine Christianity asks of us if we are sincere about living in Christ. It is anything but easy. There is no need for any self-inflicted mortifications in the truer asceticism of Christianity. Facing into the depth that forgiving others demands of us is plenty, and there is a real dying to self accepting the bad feelings as part of ourselves. But it is only through this that we purge ourselves of them. We like to overlook our mistakes and the sticky episodes of life. We would rather not inspect them too closely because it is too painful to do so. Self-examination comes hard, especially the situations in which we have been hurt. We do not feel much inclined to sort out the tangled feelings that are strewn across our soul like live wires.

We cannot be forgiving, however, unless we can first admit that we can be vengeful and hard of heart. We do not even experience our own personality unless we take a close look at those parts of ourselves which we would ordinarily prefer to disown. We would rather push these feelings down or hide them in a haze of forgetfulness, but then we are only trying to bury a part of ourselves. It is from that grave that ghosts arise, specters that have power only when we leave them in the darkness. Forgiveness of ourselves, it is commonly said, is necessary before we can forgive anyone else. This begins by admitting just how complex and contradictory we can sometimes be in our personal relationships. Forgiveness starts when we can recognize the fullness of our faulted selves and the human condition and not turn away. Forgiveness is accomplished when we can take responsibility for what we are.

There is a marvelous freedom that comes to us when we have the courage to see ourselves pretty much as we are. It is this freedom that gives us the power to forgive others. That power, of course, is none other than that of love itself, the love that comes to life when we are truly in touch with the persons we are. Only this love enables us to redeem ourselves and others through the kind of forgiveness that is tempered in the cleansing fires of self-examination and self-acceptance.

For most of us this forgiveness remains an ideal that we work toward throughout our lives. There is indeed a process quality to life in the Spirit. To continue fighting, in the sense of dealing constructively with the issues of our inner transformation, is a healthy sign that we are alive to the action of the Spirit. "Only the living," the psalmist tells us, "can praise God." Only those who are struggling with the realistic experiences of personal growth are alive enough to praise God at all.

15. A CHURCH WHERE MAN CAN GROW

The Church, nearly the oldest of our institutions, has passed through most of the civilized world's winters. Its experience, when it reflects upon it, allows it to know man in a deeply understanding fashion. Now the Church is attempting to revive its sensitivity to man and the meaning of the Gospels for his life. Its greatest struggle is to free itself from absorption with preserving its own institutional integrity in order to recapture its Gospel commitment to man's growth. Beneath the surface changes of renewal lies the Church's effort to place itself again at the side of man. The Church fails in its own mission of growth if it does not commit itself to the cause of human growth.

Any organization as old as the Church has many concerns. It is hard for it, even when it sees again such a glowing ideal, to put these aside. It has just gotten too implicated in human affairs and in the course of human history, even in very incidental ways, to cut its ties and quash its traditions. This is more proof, hardly needed of course, of the Church's humanity. It is not a tabernacle in the sky; it reflects less the glints of a spiritual kingdom and more the dun-colored coating of a long life in the midst of men. It has not been exempt from the opportunities or the hazards of organizational dynamics. Now, however, rocked by the quest for a deeper faith that is evident throughout the world, the Church must review its organizational expressions in relationship to that central task of assisting man to become more fully himself. The business of the Church is man's life, to enrich his faith, to eliminate insofar as possible the sores and wounds in civilization that hamper man's life, and to support man as he attempts to achieve a freer and fuller experience of himself. After all the myths have been sifted, man's destiny still remains that of achieving full growth, of seeing through to the end the implications of incarnation. The Church, quite aside from whatever concerns it might have about its various departments and tradition-ridden policies, must first of all be an environment in which man's growth is encouraged and accomplished. Its presence is not that of a creaking organization cutting its losses as it learns how to manage itself anew according to the latest techniques. The task is at once more difficult and more simple: to create through its commitment to Gospel values and atmosphere a human milieu that is only extrinsically dependent on structures but which can be sensed as the essential mystical presence of God's Church, a place where man can be at home and grow.

The last thing, in fact, that the Church might want to become is efficient. That is completely the wrong idea of renewal. One shudders to think of a Church which has mastered the arts of scientific management. It has never been very efficient and it is rather late in history for it to start. The trend toward efficiency, a move which anyone who has known the Church very closely will not take very seriously, might move it further away from its human moorings. Its inexact management, plastered over by centuries of smooth but mysterious Italian domination, is an unconscious sign of the fact that it is meant to be a presence more than a powerful organization in the affairs of mankind. It has never functioned very well as a power; its future lies in being an authentically spiritual presence.

One could describe the Church's mission for the next century as that of being the place in which the most important values about man and his life are preserved, expressed, and encouraged. The Church could lose its museums, and even the rest of its monsignors, and remain unworried as long as it maintains its concern for man. No other organization on a full-time basis makes man its chief business. It is clear that Paul VI responded to this truth in his encyclical "On the Development of Peoples." The key word is, of course, development, a reflection of the Pope's sensitivity to the need to encourage the humanization of man and to explore and promote all the ways in which this can be attained. A credible Church does not utter pious slogans about man and his destiny. It struggles with and for him in all the fields which affect his growth. The Church is true to its commitment to preach the Gospel when it puts man in the very forefront of its concerns. It must open itself to all the sources which help it to understand man's behavior. The Church's interest is as wide as man's interests, from psychology to economics. In all these it learns something about man's battered but forward passage through history. The Church's mission is to breathe the Spirit on all man's activities, to raise him up constantly, to point to this dignity, and to fight for the conditions that he needs to achieve his fullness.

The Church has special concern for the values that are essential to human growth. These are, as they always have been, the Gospel values. Fundamentally, the Church must proclaim anew its wholehearted belief in man. Lip service is not enough. Nor can believing in man be separated from hoping in and loving him in practical and effective fashion. These are hard things for an organization to do. They can only be accomplished through its members, especially through those who choose lives of service or ministry to all other men. The Church, in other words, carries out its pledge to mankind through the men and women who represent it in a special way in human affairs. They express through their lives and actions the Church's beliefs. They reveal, more clearly than anything else, the Gospel as a way of life. These servants of the Church will not be able to speak of or hand on the essential human values until they experience them in some depth in their own lives. One of the most essential parts of renewal is the struggle to see that priests and religious everywhere are free from the crippling mythologies which have made them turn aside from their own full human development. The Church will not succeed in its mission until its servants are freer to discover and share their humanity with others.

The efforts to renew the priesthood and religious life are not, then, aimed merely at the convenience or pleasure of these groups. These changes are essential for the Church's over-all functioning. Freedom, trust, and loving service do not come out of the air; they cannot be expressed in a living and moving way by people who are surrounded by constraints and controls. The servants of the Church are not courting license, as some churchmen would mistakenly have us believe; they are forging their way toward the kinds of lives which they need in order to be fully present in the lives of those they serve. They are not trying to get out of something. They are trying to take on the most difficult task in the world, struggling with man in a practical way to promote his complete development.

This brings up a closely related question: what of all the discussion about the authority of the Church? This is a constant topic of concern in the pronouncements of churchmen. Indeed, some of them speak of this with the uneasiness of a politician who keeps looking over his shoulder to see that his organization is maintaining its discipline. This is important in the game of power politics but, even for the politician, it is a far cry from statesmanship. So too for the ecclesiastic, this kind of power brokerage is a far cry from churchmanship. As a matter of fact, the Church is not at all filled with people who are trying to destroy the Church's authority. There are rather more people anxious to understand the best way to live and willing to follow those who can assist them to discover and live a richer life. Such a life is the Gospel life, and it is not one of controls or politics.

Who has authority in the world today? This is a much better question to ask because the answer reveals clearly the human dynamics that must be understood by all men who possess authority. Authority, of course, belongs to those persons who have authentic voices, to those individuals, in other words, who speak to the experience and hopes of mankind. Those men have authority who understand man's thirst for life and growth and who help him, through their vision and leadership, to attain it. This was the authority of Jesus; it was the kind of servant authority he handed on to his followers. Obviously, this authority does not rest so much on an individual's legal right to exercise it as it does on the depth and genuineness of his concerned faith. The Church does not lack for men insisting on their rights because of their office; it lacks terribly leaders whose authority springs from their profound commitment to the development of men through the action of the Spirit. The trouble with authority in the Church is that there are so few men people care to follow, so few men who can and do preach the Gospel as a freeing document, and so many who want only to control people into their vision of heaven. The latter kind of authority is not really apostolic authority. It does not work very well and it will not work any better just because churchmen make loud and complaining noises about the lack of obedience in the world today. People respond when they recognize real preachers of the Gospel of Jesus Christ, and they do it freely and fully.

The Church is meant to be more of a home than an organization, a home because, in the ambiance which commitment to the Gospel creates, it should make room for all those who seek to discover and make secure their own identity as men. It cannot be a closed corporation, a community unto itself, a gathering of the elect who look out somewhat uneasily at all those others who are so different. This is a failed pattern of the Church built on man's tendency to turn in on himself rather than to expand his potential through opening himself up to others. The Church, if it is to be a mystical presence, achieves this as it enlarges its spirit and makes men welcome no matter what their spiritual or psychological condition is. For example, there is much talk of the need to minister to the homosexual and to others whose life experiences have caused them difficulties in growth and adjustment. The solution offered by some is the development of homosexual communities in which a special response can be given to persons with this difficulty. This, of course, is to isolate them, to separate them out from the rest of the Christian community, and, subtly at least, to make them feel more different than ever. A true Church makes room for everybody, allowing him to face his own difficulties without shame and encouraging him to try to deal as constructively as possible with his problems without condemning him. The Church, as the late Cardinal Meyer of Chicago reminded the bishops of Vatican II, is the home of sinners, and that means all of us.

A genuine openness to all struggling persons cuts across many of the other unfortunate sociological realities of our day. One turns, for example, to the difficulty which the un-

married or the widowed experience in trying to lead some
kind of normal social life. They do not fit in, they are always
an extra guest without a mate, and for this reason they may
lead crushingly lonely lives. The Christian community, if it
is in fact committed to man and to his growth, makes room
for these people, not defining them as outsiders but allowing
them to experience the genuine acceptance and confirmation
of their personalities that only a community that is filled
with the Spirit offers to others. It is the community that acts
rather than just dreams that could be the transforming force
in the history of the world. The translation of the great
themes of theology into psychological reality is the task of the
Church that would make men feel at home. Only this kind
of open spirit can ultimately wipe out the still virulent strains
of racial and ethnic prejudice that have infected man for so
long.

This analogy of the Church as a home will make many uneasy. It does not seem theologically elegant compared to the
talk of the kingdom. But it is a very real and available notion.
It is, after all, difficult to run a home according to the rules
which fit an organization. However, psychologically speaking,
the more you make Christ's community into an organization,
the less it truly fulfills its mission as a church. The more you
can tolerate the kind of fluid and flexible organization that
is needed in a home, the more nearly does the Church approach what it truly should be for all men. To put it another
way, the only institution we know in which people truly grow
is the family. The family is under a lot of stress in the world
today but, despite this, it is the only model which is based
on and is expressive of the best in human relationships. The
family creates an atmosphere of growth rather than a domain
of control. Its sense of relationship endures across separations,
privations, and even death itself. Man receives life in a family,
grows to understand his own identity, and separates himself
from his family in order to begin the process anew as his own
responsibility. The values that make for a healthy family are
precisely the values which the Church should care about if
it is effectively to be an agent of man's continued growth.
These values are almost too homely to talk about; and yet

they are the richest, deepest, and most productive of human growth of all the concepts we know.

Robert Frost once wrote, "Home is the place where, when you have to go there, they have to let you in." For a world that is longing for a place in which to rediscover its identity, this is what the Church can truly provide. A family is not an efficient or well-managed enterprise. Human beings do not grow well except in the free and approximate kinds of conditions they seem to obtain in a healthy home. It is difficult, after a short few years, for example, ever to get a family together for one meal except at great feasts. Life pulls the children away from the table into new worlds of their own very quickly. And in every family someone is always angry with someone else. One could flesh out the analogy quite extensively and yet the same point would be made. We need a human environment, that is to say, an incarnational environment, where men can face the truth about themselves without feeling that they are going to be falsely condemned or mindlessly encouraged, a place where, when men, whether sick or sinning, have to go there, they know that they will be taken in. The Church can tolerate poor management if it is humanly effective in preserving and expressing the values that make man what he is.

This kind of Church, this place that would be a home for mankind, is surely part of the vision of the Council Fathers who spoke of the Church as a mystery of God's people, a community big enough for all men rather than just for a moral or ideological elite. This Church would keep its doors open and hardly worry so much about its rules of membership and its power to exclude people. A family finds room for even its prodigal sons; so too should the Church, despite the lingering fondness of some churchmen for the notions of excommunication and other punishment. The Church can make the most bewildered and rebellious person feel comfortable because she is an ancient and wise counselor and she has seen everything man can do; she is capable of too much understanding of man and his struggles to be his stern and unforgiving judge. There is nothing the Church has not seen in man's history, few places she has not traveled with him, few faults that she has not been guilty of herself. That is what so excellently fits the Church for the role that it again has the opportunity to carry out in a troubled and orphaned world.

The Church can let almost everything else go but it can never lose sight of the fact that it is meant to be the environment in which men can become themselves, the place where men can be forgiven and redeemed, the environment of incarnation in which they can achieve fullness once again. This is the Church whose doors are open to all, the community that dies to its own selfishness repeatedly in order to share its life with those who need it. This is a lot to ask of an organization as full of years as the Catholic Church. But it is the least that can be asked of the Church which says that it is one and holy and the servant of all men.